D1004805

Genealogical Research in England's Public Record Office:

A Guide for North Americans

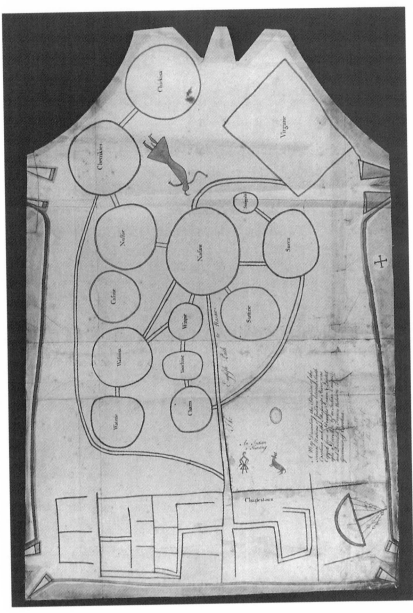

"A map describing the situation of several nations of Indians between South Carolina and the Mississippi River . . . copyed from a draft drawn upon a deer skin and presented to Francis Nicholson governor of Carolina," undated (CO 700/North American Colonies/ Gen 6 (1))

Genealogical Research in England's Public Record Office:

A Guide for North Americans

2nd edition

Judith Prowse Reid
&
Simon Fowler

Published by Genealogical Publishing Co., Inc.
1001 N. Calvert Street, Baltimore, MD 21202
Library of Congress Catalogue Card Number 99-85937
International Standard Book Number 0-8063-1632-2
Made in the United States of America

Contents

Illustrations

Preface

The subject of this book, North American genealogy resources in the Public Record Office, was first suggested to me in 1992 by Dr. Elizabeth Hallam-Smith of the Public Record Office (PRO), Kew, England. At the time, I was considering an international study experience and was examining various possibilities. Her suggestion that an institution with the international renown of the Public Record Office might need yet *another* guide at first seemed astonishing to me. After much thought, I decided that her suggestion indeed had merit, and I proposed it as the subject of a Fulbright Fellowship for Research Librarians. I was fortunate in being selected to receive the fellowship in 1994, and conducted the research for the first edition of this book at the PRO in Kew and London during the fall of 1994, and the research for this volume in the spring of 1999.

During my research, I came to appreciate the immense value of the PRO's holdings for North American genealogists and historians. At the same time, I developed a keen awareness of the difficulties of knowing when to attempt research at the PRO and how to conduct it efficiently. This guide reflects what I was able to learn through my studies. I hope readers will find it helpful in planning their own research.

Judith Prowse Reid
February 2000

Acknowledgments

Any work of the size and complexity of this one is inevitably the product of many persons. I am indebted to numerous people for their contributions to this book. First, I wish to thank my colleagues at the Public Record Office (PRO) in Kew and London. Dr. Elizabeth Hallam-Smith supported my proposal to study at the PRO and welcomed me when I arrived. Simon Fowler was my chief mentor while at the PRO, and I am indebted to him for writing chapter 2 on using the PRO, for compiling the Glossary and Appendix E on Local Government Records, as well as for hours of instruction, criticism, and assistance. For the second edition, completed in 2000, Simon has been elevated to co-author. Guy Grannum and Alfred Knightbridge helped identify additional record classes and made helpful comments on an early draft. Many other members of the PRO staff, who must remain unnamed, assisted in countless ways with the research. Their help is warmly acknowledged.

I am particularly grateful to Samuel Andrusko of the Library of Congress for his help with the index to this book. His tireless efforts have added immeasurably to its value.

Numerous people read and commented on various drafts of the book. Special thanks go to Michael Tepper and Marian Hoffman, Genealogical Publishing Company, for their encouragement and sharp blue pencils. Cecil R. Humphery-Smith of the Institute of Heraldic and Genealogical Studies, Canterbury, England, provided special help. Anne Wuehler and Blair Poelman of the Family History Library, Salt Lake City, provided especially helpful comments regarding the Family History Library's holdings of PRO materials. Lorraine St-Louis-Harrison, Mary Munk, and Lawrence Tapper, of the National Archives of Canada, were helpful regarding Canadian immigration and the holdings in the Canadian National Archives. Gerald Gawalt, Library of Congress Manuscript Division, also reviewed the manuscript. Their comments have greatly enhanced the accuracy and value of this book.

At my home institution, the Library of Congress, I want to thank Dr. James Billington, the Librarian of Congress, Suzanne Thorin, the former Chief of Staff, and Dr. Stephen James, Chief of the Humanities and Social Sciences Division, for their support of my candidacy as a Fulbright Fellow. I am also grateful to the late Judith Austin, Head, Local History and Genealogy Reading Room, and my other colleagues who cheerfully carried the extra burden of my workload during my absence.

The late Mrs. Marguerite Roll deserves a special mention. Her leadership in establishing the Local History and Genealogy Gift Fund at the Library of Congress, and her generous and continuing support, made it possible for the Library of Congress to support the fellowship through which this research was conducted.

I also wish to acknowledge the confidence of the Fulbright Commission in supporting my proposal. I hope they will find the product worthy of their faith.

Jenny and Chris Long, with whom I stayed during my research at the PRO, were especially gracious and allowed me to make their Maze Lodge truly a "home away from home." Their kind support made my research not only productive but enjoyable.

Genealogical Research in England's Public Record Office:

A Guide for North Americans

Chapter 1:
When to Use the PRO, and Why

The Public Record Office (PRO) in London, England, is one of the world's great repositories of original source documents. Its international collections include records of government and law courts from the Domesday Book of 1086 to the present. The PRO is the English equivalent to the National Archives in Canada and the United States. As a record repository, it contains unpublished, original source material generally unavailable elsewhere.

Because of its rich holdings and unique source materials, the PRO may be of great interest to genealogical researchers with English ancestors. However, the PRO is not the place to begin a genealogy inquiry. The PRO is not a general reference library and does not have extensive genealogical holdings outside its own specialized documentary collections. Much of the most frequently used PRO material is available in other institutions, and sometimes other sources suffice or are superior. In addition, the PRO's collections are generally not accessible by subject, are not easy to use, and require considerable preparation to use effectively. As a result, even experienced researchers may find that the PRO is not for them.

Because of travel expenses and other costs that must be borne by North Americans wishing to use the PRO, it is important for researchers to begin by examining resources available elsewhere. By clarifying what they want from the PRO and where and how to find it, their research experience at the PRO will be more rewarding. The objective of this book is to help researchers identify many of the more important PRO records that are available from such institutions as the Family History Library in Salt Lake City, the Library of Congress in Washington, D.C., and the National Archives of Canada in

Ottawa, and to make more effective use of their time at the PRO when they conduct research in London and Kew.

Getting Started

The best way to begin English ancestral research is to read one of the useful introductory books for English genealogy, such as Mark Herber's *Ancestral Trails* (Baltimore: Genealogical Publishing Co., 1998); Jean Cole and John Titford's *Tracing Your Family Tree* (Newbury: Countryside Books, 1997); David Hey's *The Oxford Companion to Local and Family History* (Oxford; New York: Oxford University Press, 1996) and his *The Oxford Guide to Family History* (Oxford; New York: Oxford University Press, 1993); Sherry Irvine's *Your English Ancestry: A Guide for North Americans* (Salt Lake City: Ancestry, 1993); or The Church of Jesus Christ of Latter-day Saints, Family History Library's *Research Outline: England* (Salt Lake City: Family History Library, 1997). These books will point out the importance of examining family documents, querying relatives for clues, and clarifying research opportunities using published sources in libraries before turning to unpublished material in archives.

There are several British genealogical magazines. The most comprehensive is *Family Tree Magazine*, which contains a monthly column about the Public Record Office. Airmail subscriptions are currently $52.75 (surface $42.75) and can be ordered from Mrs. F. Rand, 1062 N. Buhach Road, Merced, CA 95340 (U.S. residents west of the Mississippi) or Mrs. J. Harvey, 2420 Newport Drive, Lansing, MI 48906-3541 (U.S. residents east of the Mississippi). Canadians should contact SEL Enterprises, 178 Grandview Avenue, Thornhill, Ontario L3T 1J1 Canada.

An increasing amount of genealogical material relating to the British Isles is to be found on the Internet. The most comprehensive site is the UK and Ireland Genealogical Information Service, known as GENUKI (**http://www.genuki.org.uk/**). Other sites providing links to British genealogical information are the British Isles Family History Society of the U.S.A. (**http://www.rootsweb.com/~bifhsusa/**) and Cyndi's List of

Genealogy Sites on the Internet (**http://www.CyndisList.com/**).
A number of British family history societies also have
Internet sites. A sampling of these include the Cornwall Family History Society (**http://www.cfhs.demon.co.uk/Society/
index.html**), the Family History Society of Cheshire (**http://
www.users.zetnet.co.uk/blangston/fhsc/index.htm**), and the
Manchester & Lancashire Family History Society (**http://
www.mlfhs.demon.co.uk/**).

Helpful sources for searching Scottish genealogy are
Kathleen B. Cory's *Tracing Your Scottish Ancestry*, 2nd. ed. (Bal-
timore: Genealogical Publishing Co., 1997), Sherry Irvine's *Your
Scottish Ancestry: A Guide for North Americans* (Salt Lake City:
Ancestry, 1997), and Cecil Sinclair's *Tracing Your Scottish Ancestors: A Guide to Ancestry Research in the Scottish Record Of-
fice*, rev. ed. (Edinburgh: HMSO, 1997). Useful guides to Irish
genealogy are John Grenham's *Tracing Your Irish Ancestors: The
Complete Guide*, 2nd ed. (Baltimore: Genealogical Publishing
Co., 2000), and *Irish Genealogy: A Record Finder*, edited by Donal
F. Begley (Dublin: Heraldic Artists, 1987). For Wales, the best
source is *Welsh Family History: A Guide to Research*, 2nd ed.,
edited by John and Sheila Rowlands (Baltimore: Genealogical
Publishing Co., 1999).

Vital Statistics

A second step is to search out records pertaining to vital
statistics. Usually, this information is found in institutions
outside the Public Record Office. For example, civil registration of births, deaths, and marriages began on July 1, 1837 in
both England and Wales. These official state records and their
indexes are in the Family Records Centre, 1 Myddelton Street,
London EC1R 1UW. More information about the Family
Records Centre can be found in chapter 2. The Family Records
Centre only handles requests presented in person; mail requests should be directed to the General Register Office,
Smedley Hydro, Trafalgar Road, Southport, Merseyside PR8
2HH. The Family History Library, Salt Lake City, has microfilm copies of the civil registration indexes only, not the

records, of all births, deaths, and marriages for England and Wales through 1980. In-house patrons may order copies of the records through the Family History Library, which forwards the orders to the General Register Office. Similarly, wills from January 11, 1858 are available at the Principal Registry of the Family Division, First Avenue House, 44–49 High Holborn, London WC1V 6NP. Microfilm copies of the indexes to the Principal Probate Registry wills and administrations are available in the Family History Library collection and in LDS Family History Centers throughout North America. The Family History Library is also in the process of copying the wills and administrations for 1858–1920.

Researching Published Sources

Considerable published material exists for genealogical sources for the British Isles. For useful bibliographies, see P. William Filby's *American & British Genealogy & Heraldry: A Selected List of Books*, 3rd ed. (Boston: New England Historic Genealogical Society, 1983, and 1987 Supplement); Cecil R. Humphery-Smith's *A Genealogist's Bibliography* (Baltimore: Genealogical Publishing Co., 1985); Stuart A. Raymond's *English Genealogy: An Introductory Bibliography*, 3rd ed. (Birmingham: Federation of Family History Societies, 1996);[1] and Judith Prowse Reid's *Family Ties in England, Scotland, Wales, Ireland: Sources for Genealogical Research* (Washington, DC: Library of Congress, 1998). Edward Lindsay Carson Mullins' indexes to English and Welsh historical and archaeological societies' publications are unsurpassed. See his *A Guide to the Historical and Archaeological Publications of Societies in England and Wales, 1901–1933*, compiled for the Institute of Historical Research (London: Athlone Press, 1968), his *Texts and Calendars: An Analytical Guide to Serial Publications* (London: Royal Historical Society, 1958), and *Texts and Calendars II: An Analytical Guide*

---

[1] Many of the Federation's publications are regularly updated and a more recent edition may be available.

to Serial Publications, 1957–1982 (London: Royal Historical Society, 1983).

British Isles historical and genealogical collections are so rich in North America that most researchers could achieve many of their research objectives through published sources and microfilms of original records without leaving the United States and Canada. America's national library, the Library of Congress, has significant holdings of PRO records, as does the National Archives of Canada. State and provincial libraries and archives, particularly in the original thirteen American colonies, often have significant English collections, as do many large college, university, and public libraries. The Family History Library in Salt Lake City, Utah, offers one of the leading collections of British Isles genealogical materials, which can also be accessed through its many branch libraries, the Family History Centers, located around the world. For a list of PRO records on microfilm at the Family History Library, consult Joy Wade Moulton's *Genealogical Resources in English Repositories* (Baltimore: Genealogical Publishing Co., 1988, and Supplement).

Searching Archival Records

Many researchers who have consulted printed and microform sources may wish to delve more deeply than these resources allow. For them, the next step is to examine original, unpublished records. Because of its extensive holdings of original records on England, Wales, and the colonial settlement of North America, the Public Record Office offers an unparalleled opportunity for North American genealogical research.

Principally important to North American genealogists are the PRO's records pertaining to emigration and immigration; the English and Welsh census records for 1841, 1851, 1861, 1871, 1881, and 1891; nonconformist church records (i.e., other than the Church of England, such as Baptists, Presbyterians, Quakers, etc.); records of births, deaths, and marriages of British citizens overseas; pre-1858 probate records (wills, letters of administration, death duty records, and inventories); military records; tax records; association oath rolls; maps; and parliamentary papers, among hundreds of thousands of other original documents. These records are described in more detail in the chapters that follow.

Generally, the PRO does not have primary documents relating to other parts of the British Isles, outside England and Wales. Those seeking Scottish archival records should consult the National Archives of Scotland (formerly the Scottish Record Office), HM General Register House, Edinburgh EH1 3YY, Scotland (web site may be under construction—**http:// www.nas.gov.uk/**). Irish records are available both in the Public Record Office of Northern Ireland, located at 66 Balmoral Avenue, Belfast BT9 6NY, Northern Ireland (**http:// proni.nics.gov.uk/**), and the National Archives, Bishop Street, Dublin 8, Ireland (**http://www.nationalarchives.ie/**).

By no means is all unpublished material of interest to North Americans with English and Welsh ancestry found in the PRO. Throughout England there are city and county record offices and local history libraries with large collections of local archival records. Information about most of these holdings can be obtained from the National Register of Archives, which is maintained by the Royal Commission on Historical Manuscripts, Quality House, Quality Court, Chancery Lane, London WC2A 1HP. This information can be accessed online via the Commission's web site (**http://www.hmc.gov.uk/**). The web site also offers links to local record offices and other relevant sites throughout the whole of Britain.

Holdings in these local collections include court records (quarter sessions records, in particular); maps; and land, church, and tax records. The organization of British local government and local records of interest to family historians are discussed in greater detail in Appendix E. Some local record offices have personal or place name indexes. The PRO Library catalogue includes citations to journal articles as well as monographs, but in English libraries, subject cataloguing as we know it in North American libraries is rare. A selected list of city and county record offices in England and Wales may be found in Appendix A.

A number of directories identify these repositories and provide help in using them; among them are the most comprehensive guide to the location of almost all British archives, *Record Repositories in Great Britain,* edited by Ian Mortimer, 10th ed., co-published with the Royal Commission on Historical Manuscripts (London: Public Record Office Publications, 1997); Janet Foster's *British Archives: A Guide to Archive Resources in the United Kingdom,* edited by Janet Foster and Julia Sheppard, 3rd ed. (New York: Stockton Press, 1995); Jeremy Sumner Wycherley Gibson's *Record Offices: How to Find Them,* compiled by Jeremy Gibson and Pamela Peskett, 8th ed. (Baltimore: Genealogical Publishing Co., 1998)[2]; Joy Wade Moulton's *Genealogical Resources in English Repositories;* and Elizabeth Silverthorne's *London Local Archives: A Directory of Local Authority Record Offices and Libraries,* 3rd ed. (London: Guildhall Library and Greater London Archives Network, 1994). In addition, many county record offices have published guides to their own collections (see Appendix A).

About This Guide

This guide is intended to be a general introduction to selected PRO record areas of particular interest to North American genealogical researchers. Its scope is roughly from the 1600s onward because of the great difficulty of medieval genealogical research and the likelihood that most North Americans will not have researched their families further back than the seventeenth century. Selected references relate primarily to colonial America, English Canada, and West Indies sources.

The remainder of this book is organized into four chapters. Chapter 2 provides helpful logistical information about working at the PRO. Chapter 3 describes the organization of records at the PRO and discusses aids available for locating them. Chapter 4 describes PRO records pertaining to emigration and

---

[2] Many of Gibson's works are frequently updated and a more recent edition may be available.

immigration. Chapter 5 addresses other principal record classes, including censuses; nonconformist church records; birth, death, and marriage records; as well as military, taxation, and parliamentary records, among others. Appendices identify principal public record offices in England and Wales, show a map of historical county boundaries in England and Wales, give useful addresses for genealogical research in North America and the British Isles, provide a checklist of information to have before you come to the PRO, discuss the availability of local government records, and offer a glossary of terms. A bibliography of sources and an index complete the volume.

Chapter 2:
A Guide to the PRO's Facilities

At some point in your research you may determine that you have exhausted the secondary resources available to you. When this happens, you may wish to visit the PRO to use the original records in person. Not only can this unlock doors that are hidden in secondary records, but it can provide an undeniable thrill to handle a document signed by one of your ancestors several centuries ago.

Finding your way around the PRO can be difficult, and to conduct any significant amount of research you will need to allow ample time. This chapter provides an overview of the facilities available at the PRO and provides suggestions about how you can get the most out of your visit.

> ## Contacting the PRO
> *You may contact the PRO at:*
> **Public Record Office**
> **Ruskin Avenue**
> **Kew, Richmond,**
> **Surrey TW9 4DU**
> **England**
> **Phone: 011-44-20-8392-5200**
> **Fax: 011-44-20-8878-8905**
> *or*
> **Family Records Centre**
> **1 Myddelton Street**
> **London EC1R 1UW**
> **England**
> **Phone: 011-44-20-8392-5300**
> **Fax: 011-44-20-8392-5307**
>
> *Information is also available on the Internet at:*
> http://www.pro.gov.uk/

Getting to the PRO

Location

The original headquarters of the PRO was on Chancery Lane in central London. However, the building closed at the end of 1996 and all original material is now at Kew. There remains a

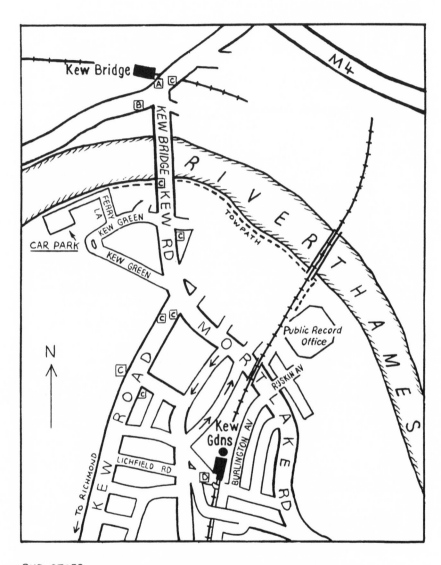

BUS STOPS

Ⓐ 237, 267   Ⓑ 65, 237, 267   Ⓒ 65   Ⓓ 391

Location of Underground stations and bus stops closest to the PRO's Kew facility central London research facility at the Family Records Centre (see details on page 17) where microfilm of census records, nonconformist parish registers, and wills proved by the Prerogative Court of Canterbury can be consulted.

Transportation to the PRO at Kew

Because the Kew facility houses the vast majority of the PRO's holdings, this chapter will first concentrate on that facility. Kew is a suburb of London about eight miles southwest of Trafalgar Square in central London. It is located near the Royal Botanical Gardens ("Kew Gardens"). The best way to get to the PRO is by Underground (subway). The nearest station is Kew Gardens on the District Line (colored green on Underground maps). It is about a ten-minute walk from the station to the PRO. South West Trains offer service every half-hour to Kew Bridge station from Waterloo or Staines. In good weather Kew Bridge station is a pleasant fifteen-minute walk from the PRO over Kew Bridge and along the towpath. There are also a number of bus routes which go through Kew, but none are convenient to the PRO.[3]

If you choose to drive, the PRO is just off Mortlake Road, or South Circular Road, and is well-signposted. There is ample free parking. Traffic can be very congested, however, and it is usually best to travel by public transportation. Maps and details of local public transportation are available free from the PRO.

Accommodations

Kew is one of the most pleasant areas of London and you may wish to stay in the area for a few days. The PRO can provide a list of hotels and bed and breakfast places in the area.

---

[3] See map p. 10.

The Public Record Office at Kew (photo by Hugh Alexander)

Hours

The Kew facility has most complicated opening hours. On Mondays, Wednesdays and Fridays opening hours are 9:00 to 5:00. On Tuesdays opening hours are 10:00 to 7:00 and on Thursdays 9:00 to 7:00. The Kew office is also open on Saturdays 9:30 to 5:00. Tuesday is the busiest day at the PRO and Saturday is the quietest.

Kew is closed on Sundays, public holidays, and the Saturdays before them. It is also closed during the first full week of December for stocktaking. A list of closure dates has been posted on the web site and is available from the PRO by mail.

Access

No appointments are necessary to use Kew. You will, however, need to get a reader's ticket before beginning research. Reader's tickets are issued in the reception area and are free. You will need to produce your passport as proof of identity before one can be issued. Tickets are not issued by post. They are valid for three years.

Kew is fully accessible for wheelchairs. It has staff trained in the use of sign language, as well as facilities available for the partially sighted.

Using the PRO

A very good introduction to the PRO is the video program, located in the lobby on the second floor at Kew. It provides a simple introduction to finding your way around. There is also a help desk in the lobby on the second floor outside the reading rooms.

The single best guide for new readers is Jane Cox's *New to Kew?* Public Record Office Readers' Guide no. 16 (Kew: PRO Publications, 1997). It costs £5.99 and is available by mail from the PRO.

If you are traveling with a group, the PRO can provide a special introductory talk. It may also be possible to have a behind-the-scenes tour. Contact the Publicity Manager for information; please provide as much notice as possible.

The PRO hosts a series of lectures and document workshops, many of which are designed for family historians. During your visit to the PRO, look for notices about forthcoming events. Details of forthcoming events are also posted on the PRO web site.

What You Can Bring

Each of the documents in the PRO is unique. To damage them is a crime against history and you can be prosecuted for willful destruction. Readers may bring in a notebook and reference books, but they can carry only a limited number of loose notes into the reading rooms. Only pencils may be used. Typewriters and portable computers are also permitted. Cloakrooms and lockers are available to store coats and other items you may have with you; these require a £1.00 coin. No overnight storage is available. Additional rules regarding the use of the PRO are available.

Finding and Ordering Documents at Kew

Before you can order any documents, you must have the full document reference. PRO references include letters and numbers that identify the class (or collection) of records. With these numbers, you can go directly to the indexes, known as the PRO Catalogue or Class Lists, which can be found in the lobby and in the Research Enquiries Room. See chapter 3 for more information on PRO Class Lists.

The PRO web site lists the times during which documents may be ordered. Before ordering documents, you must first get a seat from the long counter in the Document Research Room. You will be assigned an individual seat and given a beeper which will sound when your document is ready to be picked up. Documents are ordered on one of the computer terminals in the Research Enquiries Room. Instructions are provided on the screen. You may order up to three documents at a time. They should arrive within thirty to forty minutes. If they take longer than this, you should talk with the staff in the Document Reading Room. If you already hold a valid reader's ticket, you may order documents by e-mail or telephone in advance of your visit to Kew. Check the PRO web site for details.

Many documents are now available only on microfilm. This is to protect them from heavy usage, for which they were not designed. The computer will tell you which documents are on microfilm. These documents may be consulted in the Microfilm Reading Room.

The PRO has many finding aids, including the *Guide*, leaflets, and source sheets, to help you locate documents. For more information on these aids, see chapter 3.

Photocopies

It is possible to make copies of any documents you are interested in. The staff in Reprographic Orders can advise you of the best way to do this and how to do it. There are also reader-printers available to make copies of documents available on microfilm.

If you intend to reproduce documents in a book or elsewhere, you will need copyright clearance from the PRO's copyright officer. Normally, this is just a formality.

Eating and Other Facilities

There is a small restaurant in the Kew facility where you may buy tea and coffee, as well as snacks and full meals. If you prefer, you may bring your own food and eat it in the foyer.

The shop in the foyer sells books, souvenirs, and stationery. It offers one of the largest selections of genealogical books in London.

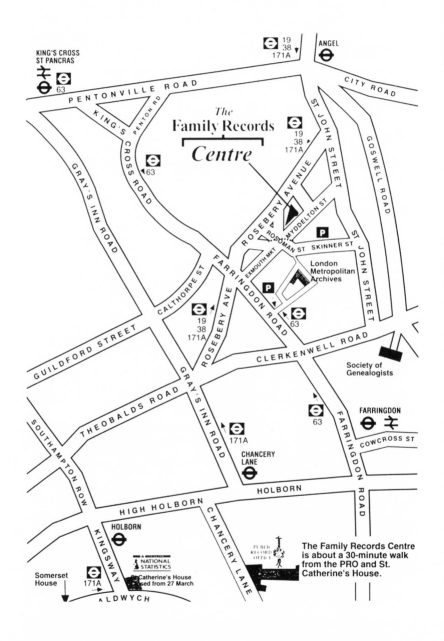

Location of the Family Records Centre

Professional Research Assistance

If you are unable to complete your research, you can employ a professional researcher to do work for you. Staff on the help desks can provide you with a list of independent researchers who may be willing to do research for a fee.

Friends of the PRO

If you fall in love with the PRO and its records, you may wish to join the Friends of the PRO, which will supply you with regular information about the Office and its records. You may pick up a leaflet while you are at the PRO or contact the Secretary, Public Record Office, Ruskin Avenue, Kew, Richmond, Surrey TW9 4DU England.

The PRO Library

The PRO Library, which is situated off the Microfilm Reading Room, houses some 150,000 books on all aspects of British political and social history. There are particularly strong collections of genealogical periodicals and books on English local history. The Library's holdings are being recatalogued and will eventually be made available on the PRO's web site. Members of the public are very welcome to use the Library.

The Family Records Centre

The Family Records Centre (FRC) has, since its opening in 1997, established itself as the most important venue for genealogical research in London. The FRC is a combination of the microfilmed records that used to be at the PRO's building in Chancery Lane and the national birth, marriage, and death records that used to be at St. Catherine's House (and before that at Somerset House).

The FRC is in the London district of Clerkenwell. It is open Mondays, Wednesdays, and Fridays from 9:00 to 5:00; Tues-

Researching census records at the Family Records Centre (photo by Hugh Alexander)

days from 10:00 to 7:00; Thursdays from 9:00 to 7:00; and Saturdays from 9:30 to 5:00. Check the PRO web site for a list of closure dates.

The nearest Underground (subway) station is Angel on the Northern Line (colored black on Underground maps). The FRC is about a ten-minute walk from Angel. The route is signposted. A number of buses (numbers 19, 38 and 171A) also pass nearby. Car parking is very limited and it is best to arrive at the Centre by public transport.

The Family Records Centre occupies three floors of a modern office block, with the entrance on Myddelton Street. It is fully accessible for wheelchairs, with elevators between the various floors, and has staff trained in the use of sign language. You do not need a reader's ticket to use the FRC.

The registers to the birth, marriage, and death records for the whole of England and Wales are located on the ground floor. A national system of registration was established on July 1, 1837 and records have been kept ever since. It is not possible to get copies of the certificates themselves without a payment of £6.50 and several days' wait. These registers are available on microfiche at a number of libraries and archives in the United Kingdom, including the PRO at Kew. It is also possible to consult registers of births, marriages, and deaths of some British citizens abroad since the late eighteenth century, including registers of deaths in the two World Wars. Also available are indexes to the Adopted Children Register, which contains a record of every person adopted through a court in England or Wales since 1927. In addition, there is a computer link to the General Register Office in Edinburgh whereby Scottish census indexes and birth, marriage, and death registers can be accessed. There is a charge of £4 per half-hour for this service. The PRO has a branch of its bookshop here, with a large variety of genealogical books available for purchase.

Census records, nonconformist registers, and wills proved in the Prerogative Court of Canterbury can be consulted on the second floor. These records are described in more detail in chapter 5. FamilySearch®, the CD-ROM product from the Family History Library, is also available. The bright and airy at-

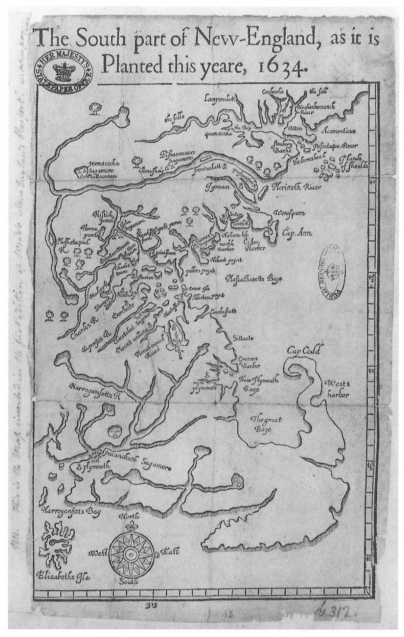

"The South part of New England as it is planted this year 1634," extract from the first edition of Wood's *New England Prospects* (MPG 312)

mosphere is very different from the gloom of the old basement in the PRO's former quarters on Chancery Lane.

In the basement you'll find lockers, drinks machines, and tables where sandwiches can be eaten. It is not possible to buy food on the premises, although there are several sandwich bars and pubs in the locality.

The best guide to the Family Records Centre is Jane Cox and Stella Colwell's *Never Been Here Before? A First Time Guide to the Family Records Centre,* Public Record Office Readers' Guide no. 17 (Kew: PRO Publications, 1997). A free leaflet, which includes a map, is available from the Family Records Centre, 1 Myddelton Street, London EC1R 1UW. Information can also be downloaded from the PRO's web pages.

Chapter 3:
Using the PRO: Finding Aids

The PRO's collections are exceedingly vast, taking in the entire history of the country, including records from the former Empire. As a result, searching for records in the PRO can be a daunting task. Fortunately, a number of general and specialized guides are available to ease access to PRO documents.

Guides that may be helpful to North American genealogical researchers at the PRO may be grouped into four categories:

- General guides to the PRO
- General handbooks and the List and Index Society's published Class Lists
- Special PRO readers' guides and leaflets for genealogical research
- Bibliographic tools for the research of North American history at the PRO

Each of these is discussed in the following sections.

Organization of PRO Records

To make effective use of these finding aids, it is first important to understand how records at the PRO are organized. The Public Record Office arranges and stores its records by a set of letters and numbers called class codes. Class codes are generally descriptive and

Important Class Codes for North American Research	
AO	Exchequer and Audit
BT	Board of Trade
CO	Colonial Office
E	Exchequer
HO	Home Office
PROB	Prerogative Court of Canterbury
PC	Privy Council
RG	General Register Office
T	Treasury
TS	Treasury Solicitor

PRO Readers' Guides of Interest to Genealogists

Cave, Michelle. *Law and Society: An Introduction to Sources for Criminal and Legal History from 1800*, Public Record Office Readers' Guide no. 14, London: PRO Publications, 1996.

Cox, Jane, and Stella Colwell. *Never Been Here Before? A First Time Guide to the Family Records Centre*, Public Record Office Readers' Guide no. 17, Kew: PRO Publications, 1997.

Cox, Jane. *New to Kew?*, Public Record Office Readers' Guide no. 16, Kew: PRO Publications, 1997.

Foot, William. *Maps for Family History: A Guide to the Records of the Tithe, Valuation Office, and National Farm Surveys of England and Wales, 1936–1943*, Public Record Office Readers' Guide no. 9, London: PRO Publications, 1994.

Fowler, Simon, and William Spencer. *Army Records for Family Historians*, 2nd ed., Public Record Office Readers' Guide no. 2, Kew: PRO Publications, 1998.

Fowler, Simon, William Spencer, and Stuart Tamblin. *Army Service Records of the First World War*, 2nd ed., Public Record Office Readers' Guide no. 19, Kew: PRO Publications, 1998.

Fowler, Simon, Peter Elliott, Roy Conyers Nesbit, and Christina Goulter. *RAF Records in the PRO*, Public Record Office Readers' Guide no. 8, London: PRO Publications, 1994.

Grannum, Guy. *Tracing Your West Indian Ancestors*, Public Record Office Readers' Guide no. 11, London: PRO Publications, 1995.

Lumas, Susan. *Making Use of the Census*, 3rd ed., Public Record Office Readers' Guide no. 1, London: PRO Publications, 1997.

Rodger, N. A. M. *Naval Records for Genealogists*, 2nd ed., Public Record Office Handbooks no. 22, London: HMSO, 1998.

Scott, Miriam. *Prerogative Court of Canterbury Wills and Other Probate Records*, Public Record Office Readers' Guide no. 15, Kew: PRO Publications, 1997.

Shorney, David. *Protestant Nonconformity and Roman Catholicism*, Public Record Office Readers' Guide no. 13, London: PRO Publications, 1997.

Smith, Kelvin, Christopher T. Watts, and Michael J. Watts. *Records of Merchant Shipping and Seamen*, Public Record Office Readers' Guide no. 20, Kew: PRO Publications, 1998.

Spencer, William. *Records of the Militia and Volunteer Forces 1758–1945*, Public Record Office Readers' Guide no. 3, Kew: PRO Publications, 1997.

Thomas, Garth. *Records of the Royal Marines*, Public Record Office Readers' Guide no. 10, London: PRO Publications, 1994.

refer to the records created by a government department or other record source. For example, CO refers to records from the Colonial Office and PC refers to the Privy Council. The sidebar on page 23 lists class codes likely to be most important for North American research; the index at the end of the volume lists the classes discussed in this publication. Each class of records is further described in the PRO's Catalogue, originally known as the Class Lists, which lists the documents deposited at the Public Record Office and gives the document ordering numbers needed to request materials. The online catalogue can be accessed through the PRO web site; a printed version of the original catalogue is available at the Public Record Office.

General Guides

Guide to the Public Record Office, a multi-volume, loose-leaf, three-part index is the only comprehensive means of reference to the holdings of the Public Record Office. Part One is a series of administrative histories for most government departments. Part Two is a description of each class (or collection) of documents. Part Three is a subject index to Parts One and Two and provides a useful, if incomplete, subject index to the records in general. A new edition of the *Guide* was published on microfiche in January 1999. Copies of the *Guide* are kept in the Research Enquiries Room and the Lobby. The microfiche edition is available at selected large libraries and archives in North America.

The PRO has issued numerous publications to facilitate access to its records. Many guides have specific relevance to genealogical researchers; these are discussed in the following sections.

Handbooks and Class Lists

The Public Record Office has also published a series of handbooks that provide more detailed help regarding specific parts

PRO Research Information Leaflets for Genealogists*

Colonies

The American and West Indian Colonies Before 1782
The American Revolution
Calendar of State Papers Colonial, America and West Indies
Land Grants in America and American Loyalists' Claims

Emigration/Immigration

Emigrants
Emigrants to North America After 1776
Immigrants
Ships' Passenger Lists, 1878–1960
Transportation to America and the West Indies, 1615–1776
Transportation to Australia, 1787–1868

Employment

Apprenticeship Records as Sources for Genealogy
Customs and Excise Records, Civil Servants and Tax Collectors
Inventions: Patents and Specifications
Merchant Seamen: Registers of Service 1913–1941
Merchant Shipping: Crew Lists and Agreements After 1861
Metropolitan Police Records of Service
Naval Dockyards
Records of Attorneys and Solicitors
Records of the Royal Irish Constabulary
Registration of Companies and Businesses
Royal Warrant Holders and Household Servants
Teachers: Using the Public Record Office

General

Anglo-Jewish History: Sources in the PRO, 18th–20th Centuries
Catholic Recusants
Civil Servants and Tax Collectors
The Ecclesiastical Census of 1851
English Local History: A Note for Beginners
Family History in England and Wales
Genealogy Before the Parish Registers
Maps and Plans: Foreign, Colonial and Dominions
Maps in the Public Record Office
The Poor and the Poor Laws
Poor Law Records, 1834–1871
Printed Parliamentary Papers

Land

Crown and Royalist Lands, 1642–1660
Enclosure Awards
Enclosure Maps

*Frequently revised, the latest text of these leaflets is available from the PRO web site.

Land Conveyances: Enrolment of Deeds, and Registration of Title
Land Conveyances: Feet of Fines, 1182–1833
Land Conveyances: Trust Deeds (Lands for Charitable Uses), 1736–1925
Manor and Other Local Court Rolls, 13th Century–1922
Manorial Records in the Public Record Office
Private Conveyances in the PRO
Records of the Ordnance Survey
Tithe Records in the PRO
Valuation Office Records: The Finance (1909–1910) Act

Legal

Assizes, Criminal Trials
Bankruptcy Records After 1869
Bankrupts and Insolvent Debtors: 1710–1869
Chancery Proceedings (Equity Suits)
Change of Name
Coroners' Inquests
Court of Requests, 1485–1642: a Court for the 'Poor'
Court of Wards and Liveries, 1540–1645: Land Inheritance
Dormant Funds in Court
English Assizes: Key to Records of Criminal Trials
English Assizes, 1656–1971: Key to Classes for Civil Trials
Equity Proceedings in the Court of the Exchequer
Inquisitions Post Mortem, Henry II–Charles I: Landholders and Their Heirs
Oath Rolls and Sacrament Certificates After 1660
Old Bailey and the Central Criminal Court: Criminal Trials
Welsh Assizes, 1831–1971: Key to Classes for Criminal and Civil Trials

Maritime (*see also* Royal Navy)

The Coastguard
Records of the Registrar General of Shipping and Seamen
Records Relating to RMS Titanic

Military

Army

Army: Campaign Records, 1660–1714
Army: Campaign Records, 1714–1815
Army: Courts Martial, 17th–20th Centuries
Army: First World War: Army Officers' Service Records
Army: First World War: Army War Diaries
Army: First World War: Operational Records of the British Army
Army: First World War: Soldiers' Papers, 1914–1920
Army: First World War: War Dead
Army: Medieval and Early Modern Soldiers: Military Recruitment
     and Service
Army: Muster Rolls and Pay Lists, c1730–1898
Army: Officers' Records 1660–1913
Army: Operations After 1945
Army: Second World War: Army Operations
Army: Soldiers' Discharge Papers, 1760–1913
Army: Soldiers' Pension Records, 1702–1913
Army: Tudor and Stuart Local Soldiery: Militia Muster Rolls
Army Other Ranks: Finding the Regiment

British Prisoners of War, c1760–1919
British Prisoners of War, 1939–1953
Civil War Soldiers 1642–1660
Civilian Nurses and Nursing Services
First World War: Conscientious Objectors
First World War Service (Campaign) Medals: WO 329
Internees: First and Second World Wars
Medals
The Militia 1757–1914
Operational Records of the British Army, 1816–1913
Prisoners of War and Displaced Persons 1939–1953
Prisoners of War in British Hands, 1698–1919
Records of the Board of Ordnance

Royal Air Force (*see also* **Royal Navy**)
RAF: Airmen's Service Records
RAF: Operational Records of the Royal Air Force
Royal Air Force Records: Tracing an Individual

Royal Marines
Royal Marines: Further Areas of Research
Royal Marines: How to Find a Division
Royal Marines: Officers' Service Records
Royal Marines: Other Ranks' Service Records

Royal Navy
First World War: Operational Records, 1914–1919
Navy, Royal Air Force and Merchant Navy Pension Records
Royal Navy Operational Records in the Second World War, 1939–45
Royal Navy: Rating' Service Records, 1667–1923
Royal Navy: Log Books and Reports of Proceedings
Royal Navy: Officers' Service Records
Royal Navy: Operational Records of the Royal Navy, 1660–1914

Taxation
The Hearth Tax 1662–1688
Port Books, 1565–1799
Taxation Records Before 1660

Transportation
Canals: Administrative and Other Records
Railways: Administrative and Other Records
Railways: Staff Records

Vital Records
Change of Name
Death Duty Records from 1796
Divorce Records in the Public Record Office
Passport Records
Probate Records

of the collections. Of most relevance to genealogical research is Ralph Bernard Pugh's *The Records of the Colonial and Dominions Offices*, Public Record Office Handbooks no. 3 (London: HMSO, 1964). *Records of the Colonial Office, Dominion Office, Commonwealth Relations Office, and Commonwealth Office*, edited by Anne Thurston, vol. 1 of *Sources for Colonial Studies in the PRO* and Series C, vol. 1, *British Documents on the End of the Empire* (London: HMSO, 1995), updates Pugh. Also relevant are *List of Colonial Office Confidential Print to 1916*, Public Record Office Handbooks no. 8 (London: HMSO, 1965); *The Records of the Foreign Office 1782–1939*, Public Record Office Handbooks no. 13 (London: HMSO, 1969); and *Tracing Your Ancestors in the Public Record Office*, Public Record Office Handbooks no. 19, cited below. Henry Horwitz's *A Guide to Chancery Equity Records and Proceedings, 1600–1800*, 2nd ed., Public Record Office Handbooks no. 27 (Kew: PRO Publications, 1998); Edward Higgs' *A Clearer Sense of the Census: the Victorian Censuses and Historical Research*, Public Record Office Handbooks no. 28 (London: HMSO, 1996); Michael Roper's *Records of the War Office and Related Departments, 1660–1964*, Public Record Office Handbooks no. 29 (London: PRO Publications, 1998); and M. (Maureen) Jurkowski's *Lay Taxes in England and Wales, 1188–1688*, Public Record Office Handbooks no. 31 (Kew: PRO Publications, 1998) are additional helpful handbooks.

Another general bibliographic tool is the List and Index Series, published in two complementary series. The current series is published by the List and Index Society; the original series was first published by the PRO as Lists and Indexes, and later reprinted by the Kraus Reprint Corporation, New York. A number of PRO Class Lists have been reproduced by the List and Index Society.

Special Guides

The PRO has published a number of special guides to research in the PRO that focus on the interests of genealogists. These include Amanda Bevan's *Tracing Your Ancestors in the*

Public Record Office, originally published 1981 and written by Jane Cox and Timothy Padfield, 5th edition, Public Record Office Handbooks no. 19 (Kew: PRO Publications, 1999); and Jane Cox's *New to Kew?*, Public Record Office Readers' Guide no. 16 (Kew: PRO Publications, 1997). A related guide is Stella Colwell's *Dictionary of Genealogical Sources in the Public Record Office* (London: Weidenfeld and Nicolson, 1992). Other specialized guides to records in the Public Record Office that may be helpful to genealogists cover such topics as censuses, maps, and military records (see page 24). Also available are a number of step-by-step guides to finding and using some of the most popular series of records found in the Microfilm Reading Room.

Over the past year the PRO has expanded its Research Information Leaflets. Some of the leaflets most helpful to genealogists are listed on pages 26–28. The leaflets are constantly updated; for the latest text of these leaflets, see the PRO's web site. The Family Records Centre has produced its own leaflets, which are only available at the Centre itself.

Tools for North American History Research

In addition to these guides, there are a number of helpful bibliographic tools for the research of American history in the PRO. Reflecting Britain's relations with the colonies from the seventeenth to nineteenth centuries, these sources include references to Canada and the West Indies, as well as to America.

Classic guides are Charles McLean Andrews' *Guide to the Material for American History, to 1783, in the Public Record Office of Great Britain*, 2 vols. (Washington, DC: Carnegie Institution, 1912–1914), and Charles Oscar Paullin's *Guide to the Materials in London Archives for the History of the United States Since 1783*, by Charles O. Paullin and Frederic L. Paxson (Washington, DC: Carnegie Institution, 1914). Care should be taken to update PRO references to reflect current practice.

More recent works are *The American Revolution*, PRO Research Information Leaflet, *Documents of the American Revolution, 1770–1783 (Colonial Office Series)*, edited by Kenneth Gordon Davies, 21 vols. (Shannon: Irish University Press, 1972–1981), *A Guide to Manuscripts Relating to America in Great Britain and Ireland: A Revision of the Guide Edited in 1961 by B. R. Crick and Miriam Alman*, edited by John W. Raimo under the general supervision of Dennis Welland, rev. ed. (Westport, CT: Published for the British Association for American Studies by Meckler Books, 1979), and Virginia Committee on Colonial Records' *The British Public Record Office: History, Description, Record Groups, Finding Aids, and Materials for American History with Special References to Virginia*, Virginia Colonial Records Project, Special Report, 25–28 (Richmond: The Virginia State Library, 1960).

Equivalent guides for Canadian historical material in the PRO and elsewhere are Valerie Bloomfield's *Resources for Canadian Studies in Britain with Some Reference to Europe*, 2nd ed. (Ottawa: British Association for Canadian Studies, 1983), The Church of Jesus Christ of Latter-day Saints, Family History Library's *Research Outline: Canada* (Salt Lake City: Family History Library, 1993), David W. Parker's *A Guide to the Documents in the Manuscript Room at the Public Archives of Canada*, Publications of the Archives of Canada no. 10 (Ottawa: Government Printing Bureau, 1914), and his *Guide to the Materials for United States History in Canadian Archives* (Washington, DC: Carnegie Institution, 1913). Additional help is provided by Grace Hyam and Jean-Marie LeBlanc's *Manuscript Division* (Ottawa: Public Archives of Canada, 1984), and the Public Archives of Canada's Manuscript Division's *General Inventory: Manuscripts*, Vol. 2, MG11–MG16 (Ottawa: 1976). Calendars of selected Colonial Office records in the PRO, including *CO 42*, have been published in *Report on Canadian Archives*, 1890, 1894, and 1895 (Ottawa: 1891, 1895, and 1896). These volumes also refer to Nova Scotia, Prince Edward Island, New Brunswick, Cape Breton, and Hudson's Bay. Bruce G. Wilson's *Manuscripts and Government Records in the United Kingdom and Ireland Relating to Canada* (Ottawa: National Archives of Canada, 1992), likewise lists PRO records.

Equally important, especially for land information, are American colonial documents, many of which have been published. For a microfilm edition of sixty-eight of the more

American Colonial Documents

Connecticut

Connecticut (Colony). *The Public Records of the Colony of Connecticut 1636–1776*, 15 vols., Hartford, CT: Press of the Case, Lockwood & Brainard Company, 1850–1890.

Connecticut. *The Public Records of the State of Connecticut*, 15 vols., Hartford, CT: Press of the Case, Lockwood & Brainard Company, 1894–1991.

Delaware

Delaware Public Archives Commission. *Delaware Archives*, 5 vols., Wilmington, DE, 1911–1916.

Georgia

Candler, Allen Daniel. *The Revolutionary Records of the State of Georgia*, 3 vols., Atlanta: The Franklin-Turner Company, 1908.

The Colonial Records of the State of Georgia, 32 vols., Atlanta: The Franklin Printing and Publishing Co., 1904–1989.

Maryland

Archives of Maryland, 72 vols., 1883–1972; New ser., vol. I,—1990—Baltimore: Maryland Historical Society and Maryland State Archives.

Massachusetts

Massachusetts (Colony). General Court, House of Representatives. *Journals of the House of Representatives*, 55 vols., 1715–1779, Boston: Massachusetts Historical Society, 1919–1990.

Massachusetts (Colony). *Records of the Governor and Company of the Massachusetts Bay*, 5 vols. in 6, Boston: W. White, Printer to the Commonwealth, 1853–1854.

New Plymouth Colony. *Records of the Colony of New Plymouth, in New England*, 12 vols. in 10, Boston: Press of W. White, 1855–1861.

New Hampshire

New Hampshire. *Documents and Records Relating to the Province (State and Towns) of New Hampshire, from the Earliest Period of its Settlement . . . 1623–1800*, 40 vols., Manchester, NH and elsewhere: 1867–1943 (vol. 23 is *A List of Documents in the Public Record Office in London . . . Relating to the Province of New Hampshire*).

New Jersey

Documents Relating to the Colonial, Revolutionary, and Post-Revolutionary History of the State of New Jersey, 47 vols., spine title *New Jersey Archives*, Trenton, NJ: 1880–1949.

New York

The Documentary History of the State of New York, by Edmund Bailey O'Callaghan, 4 vols., Albany: Weed, Parsons and Co., Public Printers, 1849–1851.

Documents Relative to the Colonial History of the State of New York, edited by Edmund Bailey O'Callaghan, 15 vols., Albany: Weed, Parsons and Company, 1853–1887.

North Carolina

The Colonial Records of North Carolina, 2nd ser., vol. 1– , 1963– , Raleigh, NC: Division of Archives & History.

North Carolina. *The State Records of North Carolina,* 30 vols., of which the first 10 volumes are *The Colonial Records of North Carolina,* Raleigh: P. M. Hale, 1886–1907.

Pennsylvania

Colonial Records of Pennsylvania, 16 vols., Harrisburg: T. Fenn & Co., 1851–1853.

Pennsylvania Archives, 120 vols., published in nine series, Philadelphia and Harrisburg: J. Severns & Co., 1852–1935.

Rhode Island

Rhode Island (Colony). *Records of the Colony of Rhode Island and Providence Plantations in New England,* spine title *Colonial Records of Rhode Island, 1636–1792,* 10 vols., Providence: A. C. Greene and Brothers, State Printers, 1856–1865.

South Carolina

Great Britain. Public Record Office. *Records in the British Public Record Office Relating to South Carolina, 1663–1710,* 5 vols., Atlanta: Printed for the Historical Commission of South Carolina by Foote & Davies Company, 1928–1947.

South Carolina (Colony). Assembly. *Colonial Records of South Carolina: Journals of the Commons House of Assembly,* 14 vols., Columbia: Historical Commission of South Carolina, 1951–1989.

Vermont

Vermont. *Records of the Governor and Council of the State of Vermont . . . ,* 8 vols., Montpelier, VT: Steam Press of J. & J. M. Poland, 1873–1880.

Vermont Secretary of State. State Papers of Vermont Series, 21 vols.– , Rutland and Bellows Falls, VT: 1918– .

Vermont. *Vermont State Papers: Being a Collection of Records and Documents Connected with the Assumption and Establishment of Government by the People of Vermont,* Middlebury, VT: J. W. Copeland, Printer, 1823.

Virginia

Virginia. *Calendar of Virginia State Papers and Other Manuscripts Preserved at Richmond,* 11 vols., Richmond: Imprint varies, 1875–1893.

Virginia (Colony) Council. *Legislative Journals of the Council of Colonial Virginia . . . ,* 3 vols., Richmond: The Colonial Press, Everett Waddey Co., 1918–1919.

Virginia Company of London. *The Records of the Virginia Company of London,* 4 vols., Washington, DC: U.S. Government Printing Office, 1906–1935.

Virginia. Council. *Executive Journals of the Council of Colonial Virginia,* 6 vols., Richmond: D. Bottom, Superintendent of Public Printing, 1925–1966.

Virginia. General Assembly. House of Burgesses. *Journals of the House of Burgesses of Virginia,* 13 vols., Richmond: The Colonial Press, Everett Waddey Co., 1905–1915.

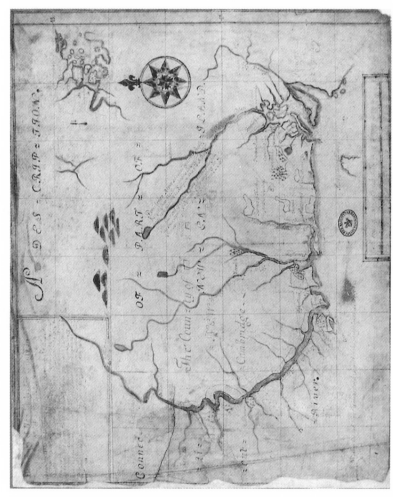

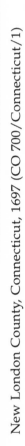

New London County, Connecticut, 1697 (CO 700/Connecticut/1)

important published colonial and state records, see *Published American Colonial Records*, 166 microfilm reels (New Haven, CT: Research Publications, 1970). Many of these records have been reprinted by the AMS Press in New York. The boxes on pages 32–33 list published documents in the colonial states.

Chapter 4:
Emigration and Immigration

Overview

Since the early 1600s the English have been emigrating to America. By the early 1700s British colonies were well-established along the Atlantic seaboard, in Canada, and in the West Indies. Favorite destinations of the early English colonists were New England, the Chesapeake, the southern colonies, and the West Indies.

English immigrants arrived on American shores for many reasons. Some came searching fortunes or new sources of livelihood. Others sought religious freedom. In some regions, especially in the Chesapeake region of Maryland and Virginia where the success of the tobacco industry demanded plantation labor, many were transported to the colonies as indentured servants. And until the American War of Independence, some English convicts were sent to America as well. Cecil Humphery-Smith's "The Nature and Origins of Emigration to America," *Family History*, vol. 5 (April 1968), pp. 163–72, gives a good overview.

As a consequence of these different methods and motives of immigration, documentary evidence of this trans-Atlantic movement exists in a wide range of sources. This chapter provides an overview of the most important, beginning with Colonial Office correspondence and registers, and including port books and passenger lists, land grants, the records of convicts, and the claims made by American Loyalists after the American Revolutionary War.

For refugees from other parts of Europe, the process of emigration sometimes involved an intermediate stopover in England. For these persons, records of their immigration into England may provide additional clues. The final section of this chapter discusses naturalization, denization, and alien records for Huguenots and other immigrants, drawing special attention to the records on the Palatines. The chapter begins with a brief overview of general sources on English emigration to America.

General Sources on Emigration

For a scholarly overview of passenger lists see Michael Tepper's *American Passenger Arrival Records: A Guide to the Records of Immigrants Arriving at American Ports by Sail and Steam* (Baltimore: Genealogical Publishing Co., 1993). P. William Filby's *Passenger and Immigration Lists Bibliography, 1538–1900: Being a Guide to Published Lists of Arrivals in the United States and Canada*, 2nd ed. (Detroit: Gale Research Co., 1988), provides a bibliographic key that unlocks the large body of literature on passenger and immigration lists. The companion list of names from Filby's passenger list bibliography is published in P. William Filby's *Passenger and Immigration Lists Index: A Guide to Published Arrival Records of About 500,000 Passengers Who Came to the United States and Canada in the Seventeenth, Eighteenth, and Nineteenth Centuries*, edited by P. William Filby and Mary K. Meyer, 3 vols., 1981, Cumulated Supplements, 1982–1985 and 1986–1990, Annual Supplements 1991– (Detroit: Gale Research Co).

Other significant passenger lists have been published and can be consulted in major genealogical libraries throughout North America. Among these are Peter Wilson Coldham's *The Complete Book of Emigrants, 1607–1776*, 4 vols. (Baltimore: Genealogical Publishing Co., 1987–1993), and *The Famine Immigrants: Lists of Irish Immigrants Arriving at the Port of New York 1846–1851*, 7 vols. (Baltimore: Genealogical Publishing Co., 1983–1986).

The earliest immigrants were not recorded by any federal, state, or local government agency and for our earliest immigrants it may not be possible to bridge the Atlantic because the records do not exist. However, a remarkable list of early immigrants from the British Isles and elsewhere has been compiled by P. William Filby in *Passenger and Immigration Lists Index* and its Supplements. This essential passenger lists series gives the names from a broad collection of published passenger lists or naturalization records of seventeenth-, eighteenth-, and nineteenth-century immigrants to North America or the West Indies.

More is known about the early settlers of New England than of the Chesapeake and southern colonies. The story of Plymouth Colony and the Puritans is particularly well researched. Charles Edward Banks' *Topographical Dictionary of 2885 English Emigrants to New England, 1620–1650*, 3rd ed. (Baltimore: Genealogical Publishing Co., 1963) and James Savage's *A Genealogical Dictionary of the First Settlers of New England*, 4 vols. (Baltimore: Genealogical Publishing Co., 1965) enumerate these English families. Two of many New England bibliographies are *New England: A Bibliography of Its History*, prepared by the Committee for a New England Bibliography, edited by Roger Parks (Hanover, NH: University Press of New England, 1989), and Kip Sperry's *New England Genealogical Research: A Guide to Sources* (Bowie, MD: Heritage Books, 1988).

Before You Come

Your time at the PRO will be more profitably spent if you are able to identify certain basic information about your ancestors. Knowing as much as possible about dates, ports of arrival, and where they came from in England will expedite your search for records in the PRO. (See the sidebar. A checklist of information to have is provided in Appendix D.) However, a large number of immigrants,

---

Before You Come

Genealogical researchers wishing to bridge the Atlantic will need to ask the following questions:

- What was the immigrant's name?
- When did the person emigrate?
- Which port city did they leave from?
- What was the name of the ship?
- When and where did they enter North America?
- What county or parish were they from?
- With whom did they come?

Answering these questions before coming to the PRO will help make emigration research more productive.

especially early ones, arrived unrecorded. There is no way of knowing the number of people for whom no immigration record exits. If your ancestor was one of these unknowns, then the chances of identifying his or her place of origin in England will be poor.

If you can identify the county of first residence in America, local courthouse records for land ownership, naturalization, wills, and probate may assist in identifying the county of origin in England. Only since 1820 has the federal government recorded ships' passengers. Those lists are at the National Archives and Records Administration in Washington, DC, and at its Regional Archives located throughout the country. They are also available on microfilm at the Family History Library in Salt Lake City, and elsewhere.

Seldom do early ships' passenger lists identify the original county or parish of an immigrant. Naturalization records may be of greater assistance in identifying the exact location of an immigrant's home; many naturalization records can be found in the Regional Archives. Staff at county courthouses may also be able to assist in identifying the location of naturalization records. The U.S. Immigration and Naturalization Service, 425 I Street, N.W., Washington, DC 20536, has records for immigrants after 1906.

The National Archives of Canada has ship passenger arrival records beginning in 1865 for the port of Quebec, and 1881 for Halifax. Microfilm of these records is available from the National Archives of Canada through interlibrary loan. The Family History Library also has this microfilm. The Ontario provincial immigration records from 1869 to 1897 are at the Archives of Ontario in Toronto.

Only a few widely scattered lists of immigrants have been identified for the period prior to 1865, generally for subsidized emigration schemes from Great Britain. Most of these are found in *CO 384.* An index to those lists for 1817–1831 is available on microfilm from the National Archives of Canada.

In Canada, there was no separate citizenship from Great Britain until 1947, and immigrants from Great Britain to Canada were not required to be naturalized. Before that date, therefore, naturalization records pertain to immigrants who lacked British citizenship. The first naturalization laws for the colonies of British North America date from after the War of 1812; in New Brunswick, certificates of naturalization date from 1817; and in Upper Canada, Ontario, they date from 1828. Laws for other provinces were enacted later. Since 1867, naturalization has been handled by the Office of the Secretary of State for Canada. The National Archives of Canada has microfilm copies of naturalization papers for Upper Canada, Ontario, for 1828 to 1850, and these are available through interlibrary loan. Donald A. McKenzie's "Upper Canada Naturalization Records (1828–1850)," in *Families*, vol. 18 (1979), pp. 103–115, and vol. 19 (1980), pp. 36–56, indexes these records, containing about three thousand names. Canadian naturalization records may also be found in archives throughout Canada, and in northern United States repositories for those Canadians who later immigrated to the U.S.

Although there are numerous references to emigrant individuals and families, the Public Record Office does not have a central index of the names of emigrants in its collections. English passenger departure lists date from 1890 and are arranged chronologically by port of departure. Emigration information is chiefly found in Colonial Office, Home Office, Board of Trade, and Treasury records. Genealogists specializing in passenger lists and emigration history reckon that most of the more accessible lists of early emigrants found in PRO sources have been published.

Records on Emigrants to North America

Correspondence and Registers

Several classes of PRO records contain official correspondence and records from the period of colonization of North America.

For information about working with colonial records see *Emigrants* and *Emigrants to North America After 1776*, PRO Research Information Leaflets; "The Public Record Office,

Chancery Lane and Kew, Some References to Emigration," *Family Tree*, vol. 1 (1984–85), various issues; Ralph Bernard Pugh's *The Records of the Colonial and Dominions Offices*, which has been updated by *Records of the Colonial Office, Dominion Office, Commonwealth Relations Office, and Commonwealth Office*, edited by Anne Thurston; and *List of Colonial Office Records, Preserved in the Public Record Office*, Lists and Indexes no. 36, originally published in 1911 (reprinted New York: Kraus Reprint, 1963).

For guidance on material for colonial American history, including Canada and the West Indies, see Charles M. Andrews' *Guide to the Material for American History to 1783, in the Public Record Office of Great Britain*. Particularly useful for identifying items in record class **CO 5,** it also describes the contents of **CO 324** and **CO 326,** outlined below. Equally important for listing the contents of colonial Canadian records in the PRO are the Public Archives of Canada's *General Inventory: Manuscripts*, vol. 2, and *List of Colonial Office Records*, vol. 3: *America*, Lists and Indexes Supplementary Series no. 16 (London: Public Record Office, reprinted by the Kraus-Thomson Organization in Millwood, N.Y., 1976). *Indexes to Reports of Commissioners, 1812–1840, Colonies*, and *Indexes to Reports of Commissioners, 1828–1847, Emigration*, are useful indexes to Canadian material published in the Parliamentary Papers, vol. 58, pt. 4 (London: The House of Commons, 1847).

CO 1 Colonial Papers General Series, 1574–1757

CO 5 America and West Indies Original Correspondence, etc., 1606–1822

These classes have information about the people in the colonies and separate classes of original correspondence, entry books of the Board of Trade and the Secretary of State, with acts, sessional papers, and miscellaneous records arranged by colony (North and South Carolina, Connecticut, East and West Florida, Georgia, Maryland, Massachusetts, New England defined as Massachusetts and New Hampshire, New Hampshire, New Jersey, New York, Pennsylvania, Rhode Island, Vermont, and Virginia). References to immigration, land grants, oaths of allegiance, and Loyalists' claims can be found in *CO 5*. Both *CO 1* and *CO 5* are described and indexed up to 1738 in *Calendar of State Papers, Colonial Series, America and West Indies, 1574–1739*, 45 vols. (London: HMSO, 1860–1994), and also available from Kraus Reprint. Brief details of the Calendar and how to use it are given in the PRO leaflet *Calendar of State Papers Colonial, America and West Indies*. The Calendar also includes *CO 391 Board of Trade Minutes, 1675 to 1782;* from 1704 to 1782 the Minutes are published in a separate series, *Journal of the Commissioners for Trade and Plantations*, 14 vols. (London: HMSO, 1920–1938 and reprinted by Kraus Reprint, 1969). The Manuscript Division of the Library of Congress has microfilm or photostat copies of many of the Colonial Office documents, as does the National Archives of Canada. Published documents and sources are available in large libraries in North America.

CO 6 British North America Original Correspondence, 1816 to 1868

This collection relates mainly to the American-Canadian boundary, expeditions to the Northwest, and the emigration to and settlement of Canada. Information about the Hudson's Bay Company is also included.

BH 1 Microfilm of Hudson's Bay Company Archives, 1667 to 1952

These records are available at the PRO, and the National Archives of Canada also has microfilm of the Hudson's Bay Company Archives. *CO 327* and *CO 328,* described below, are the registers for this correspondence. The Hudson's Bay Company Archives is located at the Provincial Archives of Manitoba in Winnipeg, Canada.

CO 42 Canada Original Correspondence, 1700 to 1922

This large class documents Canadian history and includes records from Quebec in the 1700s, Lower and Upper Canada from the late 1700s to the mid-1800s, the Province of Canada in the mid-1800s, and finally the Dominion of Canada. As is the case for *CO 6,* classes *CO 327* and *CO 328* are registers for this correspondence. *Report on Canadian Archives, 1890* (Ottawa: 1891) includes a published calendar for part of *CO 42.*

Separate classes of correspondence also exist for some provinces. For New Brunswick, see *CO 188 Original Correspondence, 1784–1867; CO 358 Register of Correspondence* is the register for this correspondence. For Newfoundland, use *CO 194 Original Correspondence, 1696 to 1922,* and *CO 359 Register of Correspondence.* For Nova Scotia and Cape Breton, use *CO 217 Original Correspondence, 1710 to 1867,* and *CO 362 Register of Correspondence.* For Prince Edward Island, use *CO 226 Original Correspondence, 1769 to 1873,* and *CO 364 Register of Correspondence.* For Vancouver Island, use *CO 305 Original Correspondence, 1846 to 1867,* and *CO 373 Register of Correspondence.*

CO 324 Colonies General Entry Books, Series I, 1662 to 1872

These entry books contain correspondence about the colonies, including land grants from 1750 to 1771 in Nova Scotia, Quebec, North and South Carolina, East Florida, Massachusetts, and Virginia. They list names of persons in the American colonies from 1740 to 1772 swearing oaths of allegiance to the Crown and becoming naturalized British citizens. Annual lists of those naturalized were sent to the Commissioners for Trade and Plantations in London and are also in *CO 5.* Montague Spencer Giuseppi's *Naturalizations of Foreign Protestants in the American and West Indian Colonies (Pursuant to Statute 13 George II, c. 7),* originally published in Publications of the Huguenot Society of London, vol. 24, 1921

(Baltimore: Genealogical Publishing Co., 1979) lists the names of over seven thousand naturalized foreign Protestants from 1740 to 1761.

CO 326 General Registers, 1623 to 1849

These records are the Board of Trade registers, indexes of letters, and minutes referring to trade and colonial papers between 1635 and 1787. This class also includes the general registers of the colonial letters received in the Secretary of State's Office between 1810 and 1849, after which date the registers are arranged by colony. Much of North America and the West Indies is included in this class, which contains information about Lower and Upper Canada, and a large part of colonial America, including New England, the Carolinas, Georgia, Maryland, New Jersey, New York, and Virginia. Indexing varies; early volumes give a brief account of contents of letters, but later volumes may only give the correspondent's name, the date of reply, and the action taken.

CO 327 British North America Emigration Registers, 1850 to 1863

CO 328 British North America General Registers, 1850 to 1868

These registers record mid-nineteenth-century emigration history chiefly for Canada. They will be of greatest use to those interested in the history of North American emigration, although some names are listed at the end of each volume. The contents are arranged by government department. *CO 6* and *CO 42* contain the original correspondence to which the registers in *CO 327* and *CO 328* relate.

CO 384 Emigration Original Correspondence, 1817 to 1896

This class contains correspondence relating to settlement in Canada from 1817 to around 1871 and contains the names of

Passenger list for S.S. *Oregon* bound for Quebec and Montreal, July 1892 (BT 27/97)

settlers, including many from Ireland. An index to lists for subsidized emigration schemes from Great Britain to Canada for 1817–1831 is available on microfilm from the National Archives of Canada. ***CO 428 Emigration Register of Correspondence, 1850 to 1896,*** is a partial finding aid to the contents of ***CO 384.***

CO 385 Emigration Entry Books, 1814 to 1871

This class lists the names of Scottish settlers in Canada in 1815, and contains emigration agents' correspondence, and North American correspondence.

CO 386 Land and Emigration Commission, etc., 1833 to 1894

This class contains the original correspondence and entry books for the Agent General for Emigration and the Land and Emigration Commission. Created in 1840, the Colonial Land and Emigration Commission was empowered to handle land grants, the emigration of settlers, and similar emigration matters. It gives names of settlers in North America and letters from settlers or those intending to settle in the colonies.

Passports, Port Books, and Passenger Lists

Several classes contain records of ships' passengers, licenses to leave the country, or port records of departures from England to North America. These records are also described in the PRO leaflet *Passport Records*.

E 157 Exchequer: King's Remembrancer: Licenses to Pass Beyond the Seas, 1572 to 1677

Passports began as "licenses to pass beyond the seas" in the early seventeenth century. A few records survive from various Cornish and Devonshire ports to St. Christopher in the West Indies (1633–1635), from London to New England (1634–1637), and from Gravesend to Barbados, Virginia, and Maryland (1677). The lists of ships' passengers' names have been published in Peter Wilson Coldham's *The Complete Book of Emigrants, 1607–1776*, in John C. Hotten's *The Original Lists of Persons of Quality: Emigrants, Religious Exiles, Political Rebels, Serving Men Sold for a Term of Years, Apprentices & Others Who Went from Great Britain to the American Plantations, 1600–1700* (reprint of the 1874 edition, Baltimore: Genealogical Publishing Co., 1983), and in P. William Filby's *Passenger and Immigration Lists Index*, and its Supplements. Lists of the thirty-one pieces of Class *E 157* may be found in *Class List of Records of the Exchequer King's Remembrancer Part II*, List and Index Society, vol. 108 (London: Swift, 1974, pages 130–131).

FO 610 Passsport Registers

Passports become much more important in the nineteenth and twentieth centuries. Potential users should remember that British citizens needed passports to visit only a few countries, notably Russia, before 1914. A passport was not needed to visit the United States or any British colony. The principal surviving records are the registers of passports issued between 1794 and 1916. They are in *FO 610 Passsport Registers.* These registers only record the name of the applicant and the place he or she intended to visit.

E 190 Port Books, 1565 to 1798

In England and Wales, from 1565 to 1798, Customs officials kept records of the names of vessels and their masters, merchants, cargoes, destinations, and duties paid. More information about these records can be found in the PRO leaflet *Port Books, 1565–1799*. Some passenger lists for journeys to America have been identified among the Port of London Port Books for 1696 to 1795. The names of these ships' passengers to America have been published in Peter Wilson Coldham's *The Complete Book of Emigrants, 1607–1776*, and in John C. Hotten's

The Original Lists of Persons of Quality: Emigrants, Religious Exiles, Political Rebels, Serving Men Sold for a Term of Years, Apprentices & Others Who Went from Great Britain to the American Plantations, 1600–1700. In turn, the names of these emigrants are also published in P. William Filby's *Passenger and Immigration Lists Index*, and Supplements.

The Class Lists are published in *Exchequer K.R. Port Books 1701–1798: Part 1 East Coast: Berwick to Yarmouth*, List and Index Society, vol. 58 (London: Swift, 1970); *Exchequer K.R. Port Books 1701–1798: Part II South-East, South and South-West Coasts: Ipswich to Barnstaple*, List and Index Society, vol. 66 (London: Swift, 1971); and *Exchequer K.R. Port Books 1701–1798: Part III South-West and West Coasts: Plymouth to Carlisle*, List and Index Society, vol. 80 (London: Swift, 1972).

BT 27 Ships' Passenger Lists, 1890 to 1960

Extant ships' passenger lists date from 1890 onward. No name index exists and arrangement is by year and port of departure. More information about these records can be found in the PRO leaflet *Ships' Passenger Lists, 1878–1960*. **BT 32 Registers of Passenger Lists, 1906–1951,** lists the ships leaving each port and helps locate records in **BT 27 Ships' Passenger Lists.** Name, age, occupation, and home address are given.

BT 32 Registers of Passenger Lists, 1906 to 1951

Prior to 1920 these passenger lists give, for individual ports, the names of ships and the month of departure. After 1920 the complete date of arrival or departure is recorded. Before 1908 the lists only include the ports of Southampton, Bristol, and Weymouth.

Land Grants

In colonial America the King granted land to individuals, and to companies and proprietors to organize settlements.

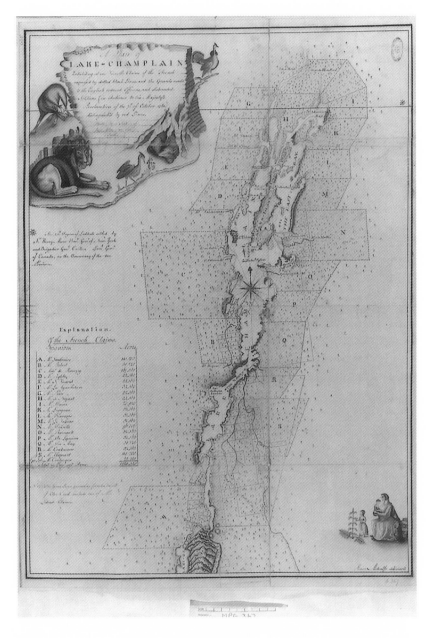

Map of Lake Champlain, New York, showing claims of French proprietors and the grants made to "English reduced officers and disbanded service men," 1767 (MPG 367)

There is no comprehensive index to these many and varied land grants in the PRO, but Charles M. Andrews' *Guide to the Material for American History to 1783, in the Public Record Office of Great Britain* serves as an index. Other references to colonial land grants can be found in *Acts of the Privy Council of England, Colonial Series,* 6 vols. (London: HMSO, 1908–1912); *Calendars of State Papers, Colonial Series, America and West Indies, 1574–1738;* and *Journal of the Commissioners for Trade and Plantations.* Details of the land grants referred to in the *Journal of the Commissioners for Trade and Plantations* may be found in the PRO class *CO 5 America and West Indies Original Correspondence, etc., 1606–1822.*

For information about Crown land grants, see Oscar Theodore Barck's *Colonial America,* by Oscar Theodore Barck, Jr. and Hugh Talmage Lefler, 2nd ed. (New York: Macmillan, 1968). Early colonial land grants in America are also discussed in *The American and West Indian Colonies Before 1782* and *Land Grants in America and American Loyalists' Claims,* PRO Research Information Leaflets. State archives and land offices in the colonial states may also have records of these land grants, and a number of states' colonial records have been published (see list on pages 32–33.

The National Archives of Canada has land petitions for Quebec and Lower Canada from 1764 to 1841, and for Upper Canada and the United Province of Canada from 1791 to 1867. Both series have been indexed and microfilmed and the index is available through interlibrary loan. Further details about Canadian land grants, with a provincial list of land sources, is found in *Tracing Your Ancestors in Canada,* 13th ed., rev. (Ottawa: National Archives of Canada, 1998). The Family History Library has many land petitions and indexes for New Brunswick, Nova Scotia, and Ontario.

PC 1 Unbound Papers, 1481 to 1946

PC refers to the Privy Council, the highest council of English government, and its records and papers contain signifi-

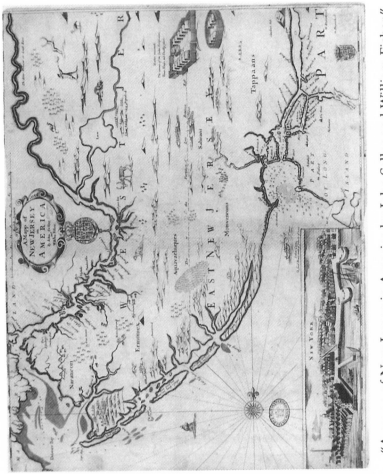

"A mapp of New Jersey in America by John Seller and William Fisher,"
1680 (CO 700/New Jersey/1)

cant material relating to colonial North America, mainly after 1700. For the American colonies and Canada, the Privy Council's Colonial Series provides the names of those appointed to colonial councils, commissions and instructions to colonial governors, and land grant information. *Acts of the Privy Council of England, Colonial Series* lists and describes this material. Three additional published references that help identify the contents of this record group are *Privy Council Office List of Unbound Papers Preserved in The Public Record Office Part 1 (Bundles 1 to 13)*, List and Index Society, vol. 24 (London: Swift, 1967); *Privy Council Office List of Unbound Papers Preserved in the Public Record Office Part II (Bundles 14 to 66)*, List and Index Society, vol. 35 (London: Swift, 1968)—particularly important as it contains items not calendared in *Acts of the Privy Council of England, Colonial Series*; and *Privy Council Office List of Unbound Papers Preserved in the Public Record Office Part III (Bundles 142 to 3020)*, List and Index Society, vol. 36 (London: Swift, 1968).

PC 2 Privy Council: Registers, 1540 to 1978

The Register of the Privy Council contains notes of the proceedings of the Council, orders and instructions, and committee reports, all having numerous references to the colonies. These may involve emigration, early residents, and land grants in colonial Canada, America, and the West Indies. Entries from the Registers from 1613 to 1783 have been printed in *Acts of the Privy Council of England, Colonial Series.*

PC 5 Plantation Books, 1678 to 1806

These "Plantation Registers" contain commissions, instructions, and orders and letters issued to governors and others in the colonial governments, and may refer to emigration and land issues. All but one of the sixteen volumes are indexed and the information from the volumes is included in *Acts of the Privy Council of England, Colonial Series.*

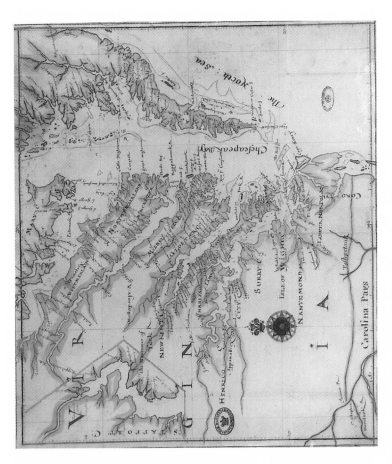

Map of part of Virginia and Maryland, including land around Chesapeake
Bay, 1681 (MPG 375)

TS 12 Treasury Solicitor and HM Procurator General: Bona Vacantia, West New Jersey Society Records, 1658 to 1921

The West New Jersey Society was formed to purchase and divide sixteen hundred parts of land in West and East New Jersey, Pennsylvania, and New England as shares for adventurers and their heirs. Society records encompass original and draft letters, entry books, minute books of its court and committee, ledgers and accounts, registers of the transfer of shares, maps and plans, original deeds and charters, a history of the Society, and miscellaneous papers about important claims. Map folders **MPD 167** and **MPD 168** contain a map of Pennsylvania, New Jersey, New York and Delaware by Lewis Evans, 1749, and other maps of New Jersey and Pennsylvania, 1774 to 1775, including a plan of Vincent Township by Anthony Wayne. A piece list of the one hundred packets is recorded in *Treasury Solicitor and H.M. Procurator General Class List: Part I (TS 1–10; 12; 14–19)*, List and Index Society, vol. 147 (London: List and Index Society, 1978, pp. 27–36).

Convicts and Bonded Emigrants Transported to America

During colonial times, bonded servants, usually between the ages of 15 and 21, were bound or indentured for a term of up to eight years in return for a passage to North America, particularly Maryland, Virginia, and the West Indies. These records may give the former place of residence and help bridge the Atlantic; for more information consult the PRO leaflet *Transportation to America and the West Indies, 1615–1776*. Similarly, thousands of convicted prisoners were transported to the colonies from 1607 when Virginia was founded until the American Revolution. Peter Wilson Coldham's *Emigrants in Chains: A Social History of Forced Emigration to the Americas of Felons, Destitute Children, Political and Religious Non-Conformists, Vagabonds, Beggars and Other Undesirables, 1607–1776* (Baltimore: Genealogical Publishing Co., 1992), and David T. Hawkings' *Criminal Ancestors: A Guide to Historical Criminal Records in England and Wales* (Stroud, England: Alan Sutton, 1992) are both useful background reading.

Peter Wilson Coldham's pioneering research and publications embody virtually all extant references to transportees to America. Consult his *The Bristol Registers of Servants Sent to Foreign Plantations, 1654–1686* (Baltimore: Genealogical Publishing Co., 1988), *The Complete Book of Emigrants in Bondage, 1614–1775* (Baltimore: Genealogical Publishing Co., 1988, and its Supplement in 1992), and *The Complete Book of Emigrants, 1607–1776.* Marion and Jack Kaminkow's *Original Lists of Emigrants in Bondage from London to the American Colonies, 1719– 1744* (Baltimore: Magna Carta Book Company, 1967), based on documents in the Guildhall Library in London, provides a name index to the more than seven thousand persons transported to the colonies as recorded in the PRO class **T 53 Warrants Relating to Money, 1676 to 1839.** Included are names from London, Surrey, Middlesex, Kent, Sussex, Hertfordshire, and Buckinghamshire. The Treasury money books in **T 53** detail payments by the Treasury to those arranging transportation of bonded servants and convicts between 1716 and 1772. Coldham's books also contain the names of transportees identified in Class **T 53.**

At the PRO, Treasury records may also be of interest. **T 1 Treasury Board Papers, 1557 to 1920,** are the original correspondence, reports, and draft minutes of the Board. Transportation lists from 1747 to 1772 for convict passengers to America may be found here. For published Treasury Board Papers, see *Calendar of Treasury Books and Papers, 1729–1745, Preserved in Her Majesty's Public Record Office,* 5 vols. (London: HMSO, 1897–1903, reprinted by Kraus Reprint, 1974), and *Calendar of Treasury Papers, 1556–1728, Preserved in Her Majesty's Public Record Office,* 6 vols. (London: Longmans, Green, Reader, and Dyer, 1868–1889, reprinted by Kraus Reprint, 1974). The Class List indexes are published in *Treasury Board Papers (T.1/319– 364) Descriptive List and Index Mainly 1745–1755,* List and Index Society, vol. 120 (London: Swift, 1975), and *Treasury Board Papers (T.1/365–388) Descriptive List and Index Mainly 1756–1758,* List and Index Society, vol. 125 (London: Swift, 1976).

Home Office records such as **HO 13 Home Office: Criminal Entry Books, 1782 to 1871,** record warrants for pardons and reprieves. Other Home Office records may also be of interest; to identify these consult the Class List.

American Loyalists' Claims

Individuals who remained loyal to the Crown during the American War of Independence are called American Loyalists, or Tories. Tories who removed to Canada are known as United Empire Loyalists. Such persons who suffered hardship as a result of their loyalty to the King were entitled to compensation.

There is much published literature about the American Loyalists. There are several bibliographies, among them Robert S. Allen's *Loyalist Literature: An Annotated Bibliographic Guide to the Writings on the Loyalists of the American Revolution* (Toronto: Dundurn Press, 1982); Jo-Ann Fellows' *A Bibliography of Loyalist Source Material in Canada* (Proceedings of the American Antiquarian Society, vol. 82, part 1, 1972); Herbert Leventhal and James E. Mooney's *A Bibliography of Loyalist Source Material in the United States* (Proceedings of the American Antiquarian Society, vols. 85–86, 1975–76); and Gregory Palmer's *A Bibliography of Loyalist Source Material in the United States, Canada, and Great Britain* (Westport, CT: Meckler Publishing, 1982). Name lists include W. Bruce Antliff's *Loyalist Settlements, 1783–1789* (Toronto: Archives of Ontario, 1985); Peter Wilson Coldham's *American Migrations 1765–1799* (Baltimore: Genealogical Publishing Co., 2000), which includes abstracts of all of the 5,800 individual claims submitted by Loyalists to the American Claims Commission between 1765 and 1799. Clifford S. Dwyer's *Index to Series 1 of American Loyalist Claims: 2 Series, AO 12, Series 1, Microform 30 Reels, AO 13, Series 2, Microform 145 Reels . . .* (DeFuniak Springs, FL: Ram Pub., 1985) and her *Index to Series II of American Loyalists Claims: 2 Series, AO 13, Series 2, Microform 145 Reels, AO 12, Series 1, Microform 30 Reels . . .* (DeFuniak Springs, FL: Ram Pub., 1986); Roger Ellis' "Records of the American Loyalists' Claims in the Public Record Office," *Genealogists' Magazine*, vol. 12 (September 1957), pp. 375–378 and ff.; E. Keith Fitzgerald's *Loyalist Lists: Over 2,000 Loyalist Names and Families from the Haldimand Papers* (Toronto: Ontario Genealogical Society, 1984); William Foot's "'That Most Precious Jewel' East Florida 1763–83," *Ge-*

nealogists' Magazine, vol. 24 (December 1992), pp. 144–148; Alexander Fraser's *United Empire Loyalists: Equiry Into the Losses and Services in Consequence of Their Loyalty: Evidence in the Canadian Claims,* 2 vols. (originally published in 1905 as *Second Report of the Bureau of Archives for the Province of Ontario,* Baltimore: Genealogical Publishing Co., 1994); Gregory Palmer's *Biographical Sketches of Loyalists of the American Revolution* (Westport, CT: Meckler Publishing, 1984); and Lorenzo Sabine's *Biographical Sketches of Loyalists of the American Revolution, with an Historical Essay,* 2 vols. (Boston: Little, Brown, and Company, 1864).

Indexes to claimants' names in the minute books of the American Loyalists' Claims Commission, *T 79,* and in the records of the East Florida Claims Commission, *T 77,* are in the PRO publication *Lists of the Records of the Treasury, Paymaster General's Office, the Exchequer and Audit Department and the Board of Trade, to 1837,* Lists and Indexes no. 46 (London: HMSO, 1921, reprinted New York: Kraus Reprint, 1963).

Microfilms of the American Loyalists' Claims, series I and II, *AO 12* and *AO 13,* are available at the Family History Library in Salt Lake City and may be purchased from Kraus Reprint. The Manuscript Division of the Library of Congress and other large libraries in North America also have copies of Loyalists' records in the PRO. The National Archives of Canada also has copies of Loyalists' records in the PRO, including some muster rolls of provincial Loyalist troops in the American War of Independence.

A useful guide for using Loyalists' records is Paul Bunnell's *Research Guide to Loyalist Ancestors: A Directory to Archives, Manuscripts, and Published Sources* (Bowie, Maryland: Heritage Books, 1990).

AO 12 American Loyalists' Claims, Series I, 1776 to 1831

American Loyalists' Claims Commission records include entry books and ledgers containing evidence of witnesses, reports and other documents, the examinations and decisions of the Commissioners, and lists of claims. The Class List includes a 265-page name index, and *AO 12/77* indexes claims for supplies furnished to the army and navy.

AO 13 American Loyalists' Claims, Series II, 1780 to 1835

Series II provides further records of the American Loyalists' Claims Commission and contains original memorials, certificates, accounts, and vouchers of the claimants, including some for East Florida. The Class List has a 334-page name index.

T 50 Documents Relating to Refugees, 1780 to 1856

These records are about American refugees 1780 to 1835, Loyalists' temporary allowances and pensions lists, and accounts, and include North and South Carolina militia and refugee receipts and reports. East Florida information is also found here.

T 77 East Florida Claims Commission, c. 1763 to 1789

This record group includes claims, with supporting documents, of the settlers of East Florida, the territory ceded to Spain in 1783 after twenty years of British rule. It contains lists of title deeds and papers relating to the management of estates, some plats, maps, including estate maps, topographical maps of East Florida, and original plans showing individual land grants. Relevant map classes are *MPD 1, MPD 2, MPD 3,* and *MPD 4.* Claimants found here were often American Loyalist claimants as well. The Class List has a name index, and *ZBOX 2/12,* ordered as a document, contains lists and indexes, including names. Wilbur Henry Siebert's *Loyalists in East Florida, 1774 to 1785; the Most Important Documents Pertaining Thereto, Edited with an Accompanying Narrative by Wilbur Henry Siebert. With a New Introd. and Pref. by George Athan Billias,* 2 vols. (Boston: Gregg Press, 1972, originally published 1929 in Deland, FL by The Florida State Historical Society), will shed further light on record group *T 77.*

T 79 American Loyalists' Claims Commission, 1777 to 1841

This record group has papers concerning the claims of American Loyalists and records of the Commissioners who were dealing with claims of Loyalists and of British merchants. It duplicates and extends from 1777 to 1812 information from the AO series and lists claimants' papers for 1784 to 1804 and 1777 to 1783. The Class List has a name index.

WO 42 Certificates of Birth, etc., 1755 to 1908

Certificates of birth, baptism, marriage, and death for a number of officers in Loyalists' American and Canadian units from 1776 to 1881 are in *WO 42/59–63.* A name index accompanies the *WO 42* Class List. Microfilm of *WO 42* is at the Family History Library.

Records on Immigrants to England

Refugees often came to England to escape religious and political persecution and to search for a better life. Those who continued their search by going to North America are of the greatest interest to American and Canadian genealogical researchers. Among the many groups who made their way to England are the Belgians, French, and Prussians, who immigrated in the 1830s and 1840s, Italians around 1860, and Chinese in the 1880s and 1890s. In addition to these are Jewish and other immigrants arriving before both World War I and World War II.

Information can be obtained from various classes of records but principally in the Home Office records on immigration (*HO 1–5,* described in this section) and Board of Trade records on passenger lists (*BT 27 and 32*). There is no composite index of names. The PRO records for immigration by Palatines are highlighted below, but if your ancestors were Huguenots, Jews, or from other groups immigrating to England from elsewhere, you may also need to learn about the immigrants' records in the PRO. The Family History Library in Salt Lake City has microfilm of much of the PRO's naturalization and denization records and indexes. The PRO leaflet *Immigrants* is a useful finding aid to this subject.

Naturalization

Between 1708 and 1711, all foreign Protestants in England who took the oaths of allegiance to the Crown and the Anglican Church became naturalized citizens. These records have been indexed and published by the Huguenot Society in William Page's *Letters of Denization and Naturalization for Aliens in England, 1509–1603* (Publications of the Huguenot Society of London, vol. 8, 1893); William A. Shaw's *Letters of Denization and Acts of Naturalization for Aliens in England and Ireland, 1603–1700* (Publications of the Huguenot Society of London, vol. 18, 1911); his *Letters of Denization and Acts of Naturalization for Aliens in England and Ireland, 1701–1800* (Publications of the Huguenot Society of London, vol. 27, 1923); and William and Susan Minet's *A Supplement to Dr. W. Shaw's Letters of Denization and Acts of Naturalization* (Publications of the Huguenot Society of London, vol. 35, 1932).

Pertinent publications of the Huguenot Society of London and other indexes to British naturalizations through 1936 are attached to **HO 1 Home Office: Denization and Naturalisation Papers and Correspondence, 1789 to 1871,** and are accessible in the PRO Reference Rooms. The Publications of the Huguenot Society of London will also be found in large libraries in North America.

Denization

An alien could gain most rights of "free subjects" by being made a denizen by letters patent from the Crown, a less expensive process than naturalization. As a denizen, it was possible to purchase land. For 1509 to 1800, indexes to denizations have been published by the Huguenot Society. These Huguenot Society of London indexes and a typescript index to denizations between 1801 and 1873 are also attached to the *HO 1* Class List and available in the PRO Reference Rooms. *HO 4 Aliens Office and Home Office: Original Patents of Denization, 1804 to 1843,* contains the original patents of denization from 1804 to 1843.

Aliens

Home Office records, *HO 2 Home Office: Aliens Act 1836: Certificates of Arrival of Aliens, 1836 to 1852,* contain the original certificates of the arrival of aliens in England and Scotland between 1836 and 1852. These certificates of aliens give nationality, profession, date of arrival, last country visited, and a signature. Arrangement is by year, under the ports of arrival.

HO 3 Home Office: Aliens Act 1836: Returns and Papers, 1836 to 1869, are returns of alien passengers made by ships' masters from 1836 to 1869 and they are bound in date order without a name index.

HO 5 Aliens Office and Home Office: Aliens' Entry Books, 1794 to 1921, contains an index of certificates of arrival of aliens from 1826 to 1849, letters relating to aliens and naturalization, registers of applications for denization, naturalization, and exemptions, and Aliens Office accounts. Richard Edward Gent Kirk's *Returns of Aliens Resident in London, 1523–1603* (Publications of the Huguenot Society of London, vol. 10, 1900–1908), is a published list.

Palatines

Individuals from the Palatinate or German Rhine region who emigrated to the American colonies can sometimes be traced through records in the PRO. The names of the Palatines who emigrated to America by way of Holland and England in 1709 are found in several classes of records in the PRO. They are also listed in Walter Allen Knittle's *Early Eighteenth Century Palatine Emigration*, originally published in 1937 (reprinted Baltimore: Genealogical Publishing Co., 1970); in a series of articles entitled "Lists of Germans from the Palatinate Who Came to England in 1709," *New York Genealogical and Biographical Record*, vols. 40–41 (1909–1910); and in Lou D. MacWethy's *The Book of Names Especially Relating to the Early Palatines and the First Settlers in the Mohawk Valley*, originally published in 1933 (reprinted Baltimore: Genealogical Publishing Co., 1969).

Chapter 5:
Other Records

The PRO collections include a wide array of other records that can help with documenting the lives of ancestors. These include censuses; birth, marriage, death, military, and tax records; and other records of governmental actions. In addition to these, a variety of special records may help document the lives of English ancestors. This chapter provides an overview of these record classes and describes reference tools that can facilitate their use.

Censuses 1841 to 1901

Decennial census returns for England, Wales, the Isle of Man, and the Channel Islands are some of the most important modern genealogical sources in the PRO. Since 1801, every ten years, a census of the population of the United Kingdom has been taken. While the names of all individuals began to be recorded in 1841, it is not until the 1851 English census that the recorded information is precise enough to be of much help to genealogists. Starting in 1851,

Record Classes for Census Records	
Date	Class
June 6, 1841	*HO 107*
March 30, 1851	*HO 107*
April 7, 1861	*RG 9*
April 2, 1871	*RG 10*
April 3, 1881	*RG 11*
April 5, 1891	*RG 12*
March 31, 1901	*RG 13*

the English censuses provide name, address, age, marital status, relationship to the head of household, sex, occupation, and parish and county of birth for each individual. The most striking difference between American and English cen-

Census document for Queen Victoria (WO 362/742)

suses is the latter's comparative lack of name indexes. American censuses are indexed by a variety of all-state name indexes so that researchers who do not know the county of origin can often identify it from the index. In England, the lack of similar indexes means a census researcher must know a place, and in large cities, an address, in order to find the records of their ancestor. Name indexes have been prepared for most of the landmark 1851 census and for all of the 1881 census. Incomplete name indexes exist for other censuses.

If your English ancestor emigrated to North America in the mid-nineteenth century or later, a search of the English censuses is recommended. At the PRO's Family Records Centre there is a Census Room for using the census microfilm. The 1881 census is now also available on microfiche and compact disc (CD). In addition, there is a CD of the 1851 census for the counties of Norfolk, Devon, and Warwickshire. The PRO has plans to digitize the 1901 census returns and make them available electronically via the Internet, as well as on microfiche; they will be accessible online at the Family Records Centre by the first working day of 2002. More information on the 1901 census is available from the PRO web site. The Family History Library in Salt Lake City has microfilm of all the available English censuses and indexes. These can also be borrowed through the Family History Centers. The PRO can do some limited searching for you; contact them for details.

Some useful guides are Jeremy Sumner Wycherley Gibson's *Census Returns 1841–1881 in Microform: A Directory to Local Holdings in Great Britain*, 6th ed. (Baltimore: Genealogical Publishing Co., 1997); Edward Higgs' *A Clearer Sense of the Census*; and Susan Lumas' *Making Use of the Census*, 3rd ed. A useful free leaflet, *Censuses of Population 1801–1891*, is available from the Family Records Centre.

Vital Statistics in Nonconformist Church Records

A nonconformist is someone who is not a member of the Church of England, the established state church in England. The PRO has a collection of nonconformist church registers that date from 1567 to 1970, but primarily cover 1775–1837. For the most part, they represent the Society of Friends or Quakers, Presbyterians, Independents or Congregationalists, Baptists, Methodists (Wesleyan and others), Huguenots, and Moravians, as well as a few other foreign churches. The PRO also has a few Catholic church registers, mainly from the north of England. Information found in the nonconformist records varies and may include births, baptisms, deaths, burials, and marriages, although by law from 1754 marriages could only be performed in the parish, or Anglican Church. Quakers and Jews were exempt.

Some nonconformist registers remain with the churches or may be in local record offices or at denominational archives and libraries. The Huguenot Society of Great Britain and Ireland has published its church registers in a monograph series which can be found in many large libraries in North America. Since 1905, the Catholic Record Society has published Catholic records; their publications are available in large libraries. Help in identifying and understanding nonconformist records can be found in Geoffrey R. Breed's *My Ancestors Were Baptists* (London: Society of Genealogists, 1988); Dr. Williams' Trust, *Nonconformist Congregations in Great Britain: A List of Histories and Other Material in Dr. Williams' Library* (London: Dr. Williams' Trust, 1973); *General Register Office List of Non-Parochial Registers: Main Series & Society of Friends Series*, List and Index Society, vol. 42 (London: Swift, 1969); William Leary's *My Ancestors Were Methodists,* 2nd ed. (London: Society of Genealogists, 1990); Edward H. Milligan and Malcolm J. Thomas' *My Ancestors Were Quakers* (London: Society of Genealogists, 1983); Patrick T. R. Palgrave-Moore's *Understanding the History and Records of Nonconformity*, 2nd ed. (Norwich, England: 1989); *The Phillimore Atlas and Index of Parish Registers*, edited by Cecil R. Humphery-Smith, New ed. (Chichester, Sussex: Phillimore & Co., 1995); *Family History in England and Wales*, PRO's Research Information Leaflet; David Shorney's *Protestant Nonconformity and Roman Catholicism;* Donald J. Steel's *Sources for Nonconformist Genealogy and Family History*, National Index of Parish Registers, vol. 2 (London: Published for the Society of Genealogists by Phillimore & Co., 1973); Donald J. Steel's *General Sources of Births, Marriages, and Deaths Before 1837*, National Index of Parish Registers, vol. 1, 1968; and Donald J. Steel and Edgar Roy Samuel's *Sources for Roman Catholic and Jewish Genealogy and Family History*, National Index of Parish Registers, vol. 3, 1974.

RG 4 General Register Office: Registers of Births, Marriages and Deaths Surrendered to the Non-Parochial Registers Commissions of 1837 and 1857, 1567 to 1858

This record class contains most of the nonconformist registers, which are accessible on microfilm at the PRO's Family Records Centre and in the Microfilm Reading Room at the PRO, Kew. *RG 4* has been indexed in the International Genealogical Index™ (IGI), the vast name index created by The Church of Jesus Christ of Latter-day Saints. The IGI is widely available at the Family History Library in Salt Lake City, the Family History Centers, at many public libraries around the world, on microfiche, and over the Internet at **http://www.familysearch.org/**. It is also available as a CD-ROM product on FamilySearch®, the computerized system from the Family History Library, which also includes the Family History Library Catalog™, Social Security Death Index, Military Index of U.S. war dead from Korea and Vietnam, and the Ancestral File™, which gives family history and pedigree information for millions of persons linked to family groups.

RG 8 General Register Office: Registers of Births, Marriages and Deaths Surrendered to the Non-Parochial Registers Commission of 1857, and Other Registers and Church Records, 1646 to 1970

This class, also available on microfilm, has fewer records than *RG 4* and is not centrally indexed.

RG 6 General Register Office: Society of Friends' Registers and Certificates of Births, Marriages and Burials, 1613 to 1841

English and Welsh Quaker records of births, deaths, burials, and marriages through 1841 are in this record class. The name indexes to the Quaker registers are not in the PRO's Family Records Centre, but are nearby in the Quaker Library at the Friends' House, Euston Road, London NW1 2BJ. These English and Welsh Quaker vital records have been microfilmed by World Microfilms, London, and are available at the Library of Congress and other large institutions as the *Friends House Library Digest Registers of Births, Marriages, and Burials for England and Wales, 17th c.–1837* (London: World Microfilms Publications, 1989). Some of these records have also been incorporated in the International Genealogical Index™ (IGI).

Birth, Death, and Marriage Records

Civil registration of births, deaths, and marriages began in 1837 in England and Wales, and these official state records and their indexes are available at the Family Records Centre, London. Copies of the registers between 1837 and 1992 are available on microfiche in the Microfilm Reading Room at the PRO, Kew. The Family Records Centre has many vital records, including military registers from regimental lists and marine birth and death records, but not all records of overseas registration. While the PRO is not the right place to begin tracing the record of an overseas birth, death, or marriage, the PRO has some vital records for British nationals entered at British embassies and consulates or of those serving at sea or in the military. *Family History in England and Wales*, PRO Research Information Leaflet, highlights both nonconformist church records and vital records for the British overseas.

Some records for the army at the PRO also contain details on baptisms and marriages, but it is necessary to know the name of the regiment to access them. The sources cited below for military records give details.

Birth, Death, and Marriage Records of the British Overseas

RG 32 Miscellaneous Foreign Returns, 1831 to 1961, RG 33 Miscellaneous Foreign Registers and Returns, 1627 to 1958, RG 34 Miscellaneous Foreign Marriages, 1826 to 1921, and *RG 35 Miscellaneous Foreign Deaths, 1830 to 1921,* contain birth, death, and marriage records for the British overseas, formerly held at the General Register Office. *RG 36 Registers*

Records of British Births, Marriages, and Deaths in the United States of America

Aberdeen, Washington: births 1916; deaths 1914	FO 700/22–23
Boston, Massachusetts: births 1871–1932; deaths 1902–1930	FO 706/1–3
Cincinnati, Ohio: births 1929, 1943–1948, 1951–1958; deaths 1947, 1950–1955	FO 700/31–35
Cleveland, Ohio: births 1914–1930, 1944–1969; deaths 1948–1969	FO 700/36–43
Dallas, Texas: births 1951–1954; deaths 1951	FO 700/24–25
Detroit, Michigan: births 1910–1969; marriages 1936–1937; deaths 1931–1945, 1949–1968	FO 700/44–53
El Paso, Texas: births 1916–1930; deaths 1914–1926	FO 700/26–27
Galveston, Texas: births 1838–1918; deaths 1850–1927	FO 701/23–24
Hawaii: births 1848–1893	FO 331/59
marriages 1850–1853	RG 33/155
Kansas City, Missouri: births 1904–1922, 1944–1966; marriages 1958–1961; deaths 1920–1926, 1943–1949, 1952–1965	FO 700/54–60
Omaha, Nebraska: births 1906	FO 700/61
Pensacola, Florida: births 1880–1901; deaths 1879–1905	FO 885/1–2
Pittsburgh, Pennsylvania: births 1954–1956	FO 700/63
Portland, Oregon: births 1880–1926; deaths 1929	FO 707/1–2
Providence, Rhode Island: births 1902–1930; deaths 1920	FO 700/8–9
St. Paul, Minnesota: births 1943–1966; deaths 1944	FO 700/71–74
Tacoma, Washington: births 1896–1921; deaths 1892–1907	FO 700/20–21

and Returns of Births, Marriages, Deaths in the Protectorates, etc. of Africa and Asia, 1895 to 1965, is another foreign register in the PRO. Indexing to ***RG 32*** through ***RG 36*** is found in ***RG 43 Miscellaneous Foreign Returns of Births, Marriages, and Deaths: Indexes, 1627 to 1960,*** arranged first by country and then name. It is available on microfilm at the PRO. Countries included are listed in *Tracing Your Ancestors in the Public Record Office* and Geoffrey Yeo's *The British Overseas: A Guide to Records of Their Births, Baptisms, Marriages, Deaths, and Burials, Available in the United Kingdom,* 2nd ed., Guildhall Library Research Guide 2 (London: Guildhall Library, 1988). Registrations entered at British embassies and consulates are found in several classes of Foreign Office records, such as ***FO 700 Embassy and Consular Archives United States of America: Various Consulates, 1880 to 1969*** (see table on page 71).

Births, Deaths, and Marriages at Sea

The PRO also has records of births, deaths, and marriages at sea in the records of the Registrar General of Shipping and Seamen. ***BT 158 Registrar General of Shipping and Seamen, Registers of Births, Deaths, and Marriages of Passengers at Sea, 1854 to 1890, BT 159 Registrar General of Shipping and Seamen, Registers of Deaths at Sea of British Nationals, 1875 to 1888, and BT 160 Registrar General of Shipping and Seamen, Registers of Births at Sea of British Nationals, 1875 to 1891,*** are at the PRO and largely duplicate the marine registers in the Family Records Centre. The latter's indexes should be consulted before trying to access the PRO's BT registers of births, deaths, and marriages at sea. ***BT 334 Registers and Indexes of Births, Marriages, and Deaths of Passengers and Seamen at Sea*** have recently been transferred to the Public Record Office. These records cover the period 1891–1972. *Records of the Registrar General of Shipping and Seamen,* PRO Research Information Leaflet, discusses these Board of Trade records. Also helpful is Kelvin Smith, Christopher T. Watts, and Michael J. Watts' *Records of Merchant Shipping and Seamen.* The Family History Library has these records on microfilm.

Probate, Wills, and Other Death Records

Records pertaining to transfers of property at death are a rich source of genealogical information for English ancestors. The PRO's collections in this area are extensive and include wills and probate records, letters of administration, will inventories, and death duty registers. These are discussed in the following sections.

Wills and Letters of Administration

Wills and letters of administration (granted to the next of kin to distribute the estate when no will was made), dating before January 11, 1858, for the Prerogative Court of Canterbury (PCC), are available at the Family Records Centre. Inventories listing the deceased's belongings from 1666 to 1730 in the PCC and death duty records from 1796 to 1904 are also available at the Family Records Centre. The latter provides a countrywide probate index from 1796 to 1858 and supplements information found in wills and letters of administration. Wills after January 11, 1858, are at the Principal Registry of the Family Division, First Avenue House, 44-49, High Holborn, London WC1V 6NP. Indexes to wills between 1858 and 1946 are available on microfiche in the Microfilm Reading Room at the PRO, Kew.

Searching for a pre-1858 probated will or letter of administration requires identifying the court in which the grant was made. The two provincial courts were the Prerogative Court of Canterbury, for southern England, and the Prerogative Court of York for the North, whose records are at the Borthwick Institute of Historical Research, St. Anthony's Hall, Peasholme Green, York YO1 2PW England. Property held in all parts of England belonging to individuals dying overseas was probated in the PCC as recorded in Peter Wilson Coldham's *American Wills and Administrations in the Prerogative Court of Canterbury, 1610–1857* (Baltimore: Genealogical Publishing Co., 1989). Also see his *American Wills Proved in London, 1611–1775* (Baltimore: Genealogical Publishing Co.,

1992). Records of the minor probate courts are deposited in county record offices or other local repositories. Anthony J. Camp's *Wills and Their Whereabouts* (London: Society of Genealogists, 1974) and Jeremy Sumner Wycherley Gibson's *Probate Jurisdictions: Where to Look for Wills*, 4th ed. (Baltimore: Genealogical Publishing Co., 1997) are essential guides for locating wills.

Class **PROB,** the records of the Prerogative Court of Canterbury, contains fifty-seven record classes. For detailed assistance consult the *Guide;* the PRO Catalogue (Class Lists); *Probate Records: Where to Look for a Will or Grant of Administration*, PRO Research Information Leaflet; Jane Cox and Stella Colwell's *Never Been Here Before? A Genealogists' Guide to the Family Records Centre;* and Jane Cox's *Wills, Inventories and Death Duties: The Records of the Prerogative Court of Canterbury and the Estate Duty Office, A Provisional Guide* (London: PRO, 1988). Further help is available from Miriam Scott's *Prerogative Court of Canterbury Wills and Other Probate Records* and from the useful free leaflet *Wills and Probate Records—Where to Find Them*, which is available from the Family Records Centre. **PROB 11 Registered Copy Wills, 1384 to 1858** and **PROB 10 Original Wills, 1484 to 1858,** which cover probated wills, are considered to be the most useful and informative classes. **PROB 6 Act Books: Administrations, 1559 to 1858** and **PROB 7 Act Books: Limited Administrations, 1810 to 1858** provide the bulk of information available on common form grants of administration. Indexes to wills and administrations are in **PROB 12 Register Books, 1383 to 1858,** which contains alphabetical indexes to **PROB 11** and serves as a means of reference to the Act Books in **PROB 6** through **PROB 9.** Along with **PROB 12,** use **PROB 13 Manuscript Calendars, 1384 to 1800** and **PROB 15 Duplicate Calendars and Register Books, 1655 to 1858** to index **PROB 11. PROB 12/71–119,** PCC wills and grants of administrations from 1701 to 1749, has been indexed by the Friends of the PRO, and this index is available in the PRO Reference Rooms.

Published indexes to the PCC's wills and administrations at the PRO are abundant, and the Family History Library has an excellent collection of English probate records and indexes, including most pre-1900 records. The British Record Society's Index Library Series has published more than a dozen indexes to these wills and administrations and they are available in large libraries in North America. References to these volumes may be found in the bibliography section of this guide. *An Index to the Wills Proved in the Prerogative Court of Canterbury, 1750–1800*, edited by Anthony J. Camp, 6 vols. (London: Society of Genealogists, 1976–1992), is a published will index. Reginald Morshead Glencross's *Administrations in the Prerogative Court of Canterbury, 1559–1580*, 2 vols. (Exeter: W. Pollard & Co., 1912–1917), indexes PCC administrations. John and George Frederick Matthews have published PCC probate indexes. *Abstracts of Probates and Sentences in the Prerogative Court of Canterbury, 1620–1624* (London: 1911); *Abstracts of Probate Acts in the Prerogative Court of Canterbury, 1630–1655*, 8 vols. (London: 1902–1928); and *Sentences and Complete Index Nominum (Probate and Sentences) for the Years 1630–1639* (London: 1907) complete the Matthews' probate publications. John Harold Morrison's *Letters of Administration, 1620–1630* (London: J. H. Morrison, 1935), and his *Wills, Sentences and Probate Acts, 1661–1670* (London: J. H. Morrison, 1935) are other useful indexes.

While not listing PCC wills and administrations, *A List of Wills, Administrations, Etc. in the Public Record Office, London, England 12th–19th Century* (Baltimore: Magna Carta Book Company, 1968) may also be of interest.

Inventories

Up to 1782 it was customary for every executor or administrator to return to the court an inventory of the deceased's personal property. ***PROB 2 Prerogative Court of Canterbury and Other Probate Jurisdictions: Inventories Compiled before 1661, 1417 to 1660*** contains a list of pieces and an index of names and places for these early inventories. ***PROB 3 Prerogative Court of Canterbury: Filed Engrossed Eighteenth Century Inventories and Associated Documents, 1718 to 1782*** has a published list of pieces and a name index, both in the Class

List, and published in the *Prerogative Court of Canterbury Inventories, Series II: Part I 1702; 1718–1733*, List and Index Society, vol. 85 (London: Swift, 1973), and *Prerogative Court of Canterbury Inventories, Series II: Part II 1734–1782, with Index*, List and Index Society, vol. 86 (London: Swift, 1973). ***PROB 4 Prerogative Court of Canterbury and other Probate Jurisdictions: Engrossed Inventories Exhibited from 1660, 1660 to c. 1720*** is another inventory class. For a list of its 6,416 pieces, see the Class List and *Prerogative Court of Canterbury, Parchment Inventories Post 1660 (PROB 4/1-6416)*, List and Index Society, vol. 221 (London: Swift, 1986). ***PROB 5 Paper Inventories, 1661 to 1732*** is further highlighted in *Principal Probate Registry: Prerogative Court of Canterbury Paper Inventories 1661–c.1725 (PROB 5): List and Index*, List and Index Society, vol. 149 (London: Swift, 1978), which provides a list of pieces and an index. ***PROB 31 Exhibits, Main Class, 1722 to 1858*** and ***PROB 32 Filed Exhibits with Inventories, 1662 to 1720*** are additional inventories. The latter's list of pieces is published in *PCC Filed Exhibits with Inventories (PROB 32), 1662–1720 Index*, List and Index Society, vol. 204 (London: Swift, 1984). ***PROB 33 Indexes to Exhibits, 1683 to 1858*** is a modern index to ***PROB 31*** and some of the inventories appearing in the index may now be found in ***PROB 5.***

The Death Duty Registers

The Death Duty Registers are a record of taxes paid on personal estates of deceased persons from 1796. Their chief use to genealogists is as a finding aid to help identify the court in which a will was proved or an administration granted. ***IR 26 Estate Duty Office: Death Duty Registers, 1796 to 1903*** and ***IR 27 Estate Duty Office: Indexes to Death Duty Registers, 1796 to 1903,*** which contains the indexes to the registers in ***IR 26,*** are the death duty record classes. A list of the pieces in these classes has been published in *Inland Revenue Estate Duty Registers and Indexes (IR 26, IR 27) 1796–1894*, List and Index Society, vol. 177 (London: Swift, 1981). *Death Duty Records From 1796*, PRO Research Information Leaflet, is another research tool.

Military Records

British military records are vast and complex. The PRO has issued a number of special guides and information leaflets for researching military records (see page 27). Many published works on British military records will likely be available in major libraries in North America. The Family History Library and the National Archives of Canada have microfilm of selected English military records.

The Public Record Office also has documents that give information about medals, awards, and pension records. Norman K. Crowder's *British Army Pensioners Abroad, 1772–1899* (Baltimore: Genealogical Publishing Co., 1995) indexes part of **WO 120.** Microfilm copies of these records are available at the Family History Library and the National Archives of Canada. For details on researching army records in general, see PRO Records Information Leaflets *Army: Soldiers' Pension Records, 1702–1913* and *Navy, Royal Air Force and Merchant Navy Pension Records.* Other essential sources are Simon Fowler's *Army Records for Family Historians,* 2nd edition; John Michael Kitzmiller's *In Search of the "Forlorn Hope": A Comprehensive Guide to Locating British Regiments and Their Records,* 2 vols. (Salt Lake City: Manuscript Pub. Foundation, 1988); and Michael J. Watts' *My Ancestor Was in the British Army: How Can I Find Out More About Him?* (London: Society of Genealogists, 1992).

Army

The British military kept separate records for officers and soldiers. For names of officers see **WO 64 Manuscript Army Lists, 1702 to 1823** and **WO 65 Printed Annual Army Lists, 1754 to 1879,** each of which has a name index located in the PRO Reference Room. Information about both army officers and soldiers is also found in **WO 25 Various Registers, 1660 to 1938. WO 76 Records of Officers' Services, 1764 to 1954** contains regimental records of army officers' service. Both lists, along with name indexes, may also be consulted in the PRO Reference Room.

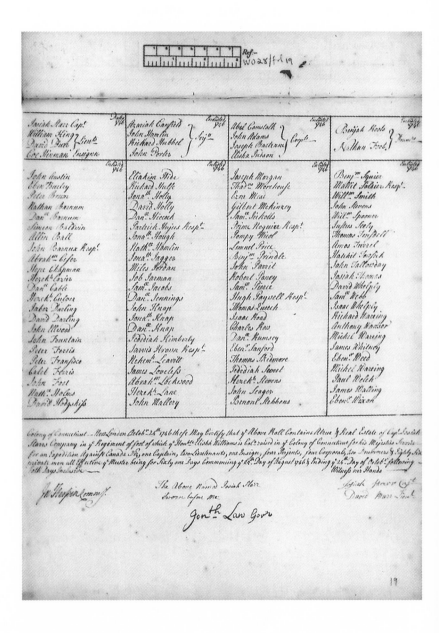

Muster List, Connecticut Militia, August 1746 (WO 28/1 fl9)

Since 1754, the official *Army Lists* have been printed. In addition, numerous unofficial army lists have been published. See the following works by Charles Dalton: *English Army Lists and Commission Registers, 1661–1714*, 6 vols. (London: Eyre & Spottiswood, 1892–1904); *George the First's Army, 1714–1727*, 2 vols. (London: Eyre & Spottiswood, 1910–1912); *Irish Army Lists, 1661–1685* (London: 1907); and *The Waterloo Roll Call*, 2nd ed. rev. and enl. (London: 1904). *Hart's Annual Army List, Militia List, & Imperial Yeomanry List* (London: J. Murray, 1840–1915) is another published army personnel list and is considered particularly useful, as it contains brief biographical notes on each officer.

To begin researching a British soldier in the army records at the PRO, you must identify your ancestor's regiment or a campaign in which he served. Records of service for soldiers who received a pension can be found in **WO 97 Royal Hospital Chelsea Soldiers' Documents, 1760 to 1913.** A name index for 1760 to 1854, which will soon be added to the PRO's web site, is located in the PRO Microfilm Reading Room. The Class List is published in *War Office Regular Army: Soldiers' Documents 1760–1913 (WO 97)*, List and Index Society, vol. 201 (London: Swift, 1983).

WO 12 General Muster Books and Pay Lists, 1732 to 1878 also contains the basic regimental service records for British army soldiers. The Class List is published in *Muster Books and Pay Lists: General Series, Cavalry (WO 12/1-13305)*, List and Index Society, vol. 210 (London: Swift, 1984).

Records for men who served in the British Armed Forces during World War I are slowly being transferred to the PRO. The estimated 85 percent of surviving records for officers in the British Army who were discharged before the end of 1920 are now at the Office in classes **WO 339 Officers' Services: Long Number Papers (Numerical)** and **WO 374 Officers' Services: Long Number Papers (Alphabetical),** with an index in **WO 338 Officers' Services: Indexes.**

Unfortunately, about 60 percent of service records for other ranks in the British Army were destroyed by fire during World War II. The surviving records are being microfilmed and transferred to the PRO. About 8 percent of these surviving records

World War I service record for Ronald Colman (WO 107/1478)

were undamaged by the fire or were re-created from other sources. These records are already at the PRO in class **WO 364 War of 1914–18: Microfilm of Soldiers' Documents: 1914–20 Collation.** The other surviving records suffered varying degrees of damage and are being transferred in surname order by complete letter into class **WO 363 War of 1914–18: Soldiers' Documents: Burnt Documents.** At the time of writing, surnames beginning with A, E, N, O, Q, U, V, and Z have been transferred. Surnames with B, C, D, F, W, X, and Y will be made available next, with the rest to follow in 2000 and afterward, concluding in 2003. Contact the PRO before visiting to see if the records you are interested in have been released.

In the meantime the Ministry of Defence, CS (R) 2b, Bourne Avenue, Hayes, Middlesex UB3 1RF England, is continuing to conduct searches of the records awaiting transfer. The fee for this service is £25. There no longer is a need to prove relationship to the person about whom information is being sought.

In recognition of the support provided by the LDS Church in filming these records, a set of films is being deposited at the Family History Library in Salt Lake City.

The best introduction to using these records is Simon Fowler, William Spencer, and Stuart Tamblin's *Army Service Records of the First World War*, 2nd ed. Another useful guide is Norman Holding's *World War One Army Ancestry*, 3rd ed. (Birmingham: Federation of Family History Societies, 1997). Useful short guides are *First World War: Soldiers' Papers, 1914–1920* and *First World War: Army Officers' Service Records*, Research Information Leaflets.

Using the Internet it is now possible to find where men of the British and Commonwealth Armies of the two world wars who died in action are buried. This service is provided by the Commonwealth War Graves Commission (**http://www.cwgc.org**). In addition the names and details of some 657,000 officers and men of the British Army who fell during World War I were recorded in a series of eighty volumes called *Soldiers Died in the Great War, 1914–19*, published in 1921 and reprinted in 1988. These volumes were published in 1998 on a CD by The Naval and Military Press, Heathfield, England.

Militia Lists

Militia lists contain the names of men eligible for military service anywhere in the British Isles and exist from the thirteenth century. Many records of militia and volunteer units are preserved in county record offices, but those collected centrally are now in the PRO. War Office class **WO 13 Militia and Volunteers Muster Books and Pay Lists, 1780 to 1878** contains muster rolls and pay books from 1790, including muster rolls for Canadian militia and volunteers for 1837 to 1843. **WO 68 Militia Records, 1759 to 1925** has records of officers' service and other personnel records. **WO 96 Militia Attestation Papers, 1806 to 1915** lists militia battalions from 1882 to 1906, annotated to form a record of service and giving date and place of birth. In **T 64 Various, 1547 to 1930, T 64/22** provides muster rolls for militia units in the colonies of Connecticut, Massachusetts, New Hampshire, and Rhode Island from 1759 to 1763. **T 64/23** is a list of officers who served in provincial forces during the American War of Independence. **WO 28 Headquarters Records, 1746 to 1909, WO 28/1, 4–5** lists men who served in provincial volunteer forces in North America during 1746 to 1747 and 1775 to 1783.

Some militia lists have been published by local history societies. Jeremy Sumner Wycherley Gibson's *Militia Lists and Musters 1757–1876: A Directory of Holdings in the British Isles*, by Jeremy Gibson and Mervyn Medlycott, 3rd ed. (Baltimore: Genealogical Publishing Co., 1994), inventories militia lists at the county record offices and lists publications by county. William Spencer's *Records of the Militia and Volunteer Forces 1758–1945* (London: PRO Publications, 1997) is also indispensable for researching British militia lists.

Royal Air Force

Service records for both officers and airmen for the early years of the RAF (up to roughly 1923) have recently been transferred to the PRO. Officers' records are in **AIR 76,** with airmen's records in **AIR 78** and registers in **AIR 79.** Next of kin may obtain brief details of officers' service from the Ministry of Defence, PG 5A (2), RAF PMC & HG PTC, RAF Innsworth, Gloucester, GL3 1EZ England. For airmen's records and officer and airmen medal enquiries, write P Man 2B (1), RAF PMC & HQ PTC, RAF Innsworth, Gloucester, GL3 1EZ England.

The PRO has a muster list of the Royal Air Force compiled on April 1, 1918, when the RAF was formed. See the AIR Class List for details. Officers' records for 1918 and 1919 are in *AIR 76 Department of Master-General of Personnel: Officers' Service Records*. This class includes records for officers who transferred from the Royal Flying Corps and Royal Naval Air Service on the formation of the RAF in 1918. No date has yet been set for the transfer of the records of other ranks. *The Air Force List* (London: HMSO, 1918–) can help trace the career of an RAF officer. Other published aids are *Royal Air Force: Airmen's Service Records* and *Royal Air Force Records: Tracing an Individual*, Research Information Leaflets, and Simon Fowler, Peter Elliott, Roy Conyers Nesbit, and Christina Goulter's *RAF Records in the PRO*.

Royal Marines

Records for the marines from 1790 until 1922, along with a name index, are accessible in the PRO's Reference Room. Consult *ADM 157 Royal Marines Attestation Forms, 1790 to 1912, ADM 159 Royal Marines Registers of Service, 1842 to 1936,* and *ADM 313 Royal Marines: Indexes to Registers of Service and Attestation Forms.* For officers, check *The Navy List* (London: HMSO, 1814–) and *ADM 196 Officers' Service Records Series III, 1756 to 1954,* the main series of service records for officers appointed from the mid-eighteenth century to 1915. *ADM 196* also has a name index from 1793, located in the PRO Microfilm Reading Room. Further help in using the records of the Royal Marines in the PRO is found in *Royal Marines: Officers' Service Records* and *Royal Marines: Other Ranks' Service Records*, PRO Research Information Leaflets, and in Garth Thomas' *Records of the Royal Marines*, an historical guide to these records.

For information about service records for both officers and enlisted men after about 1923, write the Drafting Record Office, Royal Marines, HMS *Centurion*, Grange Road, Gosport, Hampshire PO13 9XA, England.

Royal Navy

The PRO has navy service records through 1923, but tracing ordinary sailors before 1853 may be difficult unless you know the name of one of the ships on which your ancestor served. Service records of ratings, or ordinary seamen, after 1923 and of officers after 1925 are at the Ministry of Defence, MOD, CS (R)2a, Bourne Avenue, Hayes, Middlesex UB3 1RF England. To obtain information you must be next of kin and pay a fee.

The main series of service records for naval officers at the PRO begin in 1756 and are in **ADM 196 Officers' Service Records Series III, 1756 to 1954.** Name indexes are in the PRO Reference Room. Also for officers, consult *The Navy List* (London: HMSO, 1782–) and *The Commissioned Sea Officers of the Royal Navy, 1660–1815*, edited by David Syrett and R. L. DiNardo, 2nd ed. (Aldershot, England: Scolar Press; Brookfield, VT: Ashgate Pub. Co., 1994); both are likely to be available in large libraries in North America. Records of seamen are in various Admiralty records, referenced as the ADM class. Most important are **ADM 139 Continuous Service Engagement Books,** which cover seamen entering the navy during 1853–1872, and **ADM 188 Seamen's Services,** which contains the service records of seamen enlisting between 1873 and 1921. These records are available in the Family History Library in Salt Lake City.

Other records relating to World War I naval officers are **ADM 242 Records of Casualties,** a set of index cards which also include Canadian and Australian officers and records ratings (ordinary seamen). Records of officers in the Royal Naval Air Service, which merged with the Royal Flying Corps to form the Royal Air Force in April 1918, are in **ADM 273 RNAS: Registers of Officers' Services.** Records of officers in the

Women's Royal Naval Service are in *ADM 318 WRNS: Personal Files of Officers* and *ADM 321 WRNS: Registers of Appointments of Officers.*

Because of the complexity of the PRO's naval records, consult the following sources for a detailed account of how to identify and use them: *Royal Navy: Officers' Service Records* and *Royal Navy: Ratings' Records 1667–1923*, Research Information Leaflets, and N. A. M. Rodger's *Naval Records for Genealogists.*

Also of interest are papers pertaining to the Royal Navy held in North American collections. These are described in the National Maritime Museum's *Guide to British Naval Papers in North America*, compiled by Roger Morriss with the assistance of Peter Bursey (London; New York: Mansell, 1994).

Prisoners of War

PRO records on prisoners of war are, for the most part, registers of prisoners held in various depots and prison ships who were taken during the wars with France between 1793 and 1815. Included are American prisoners of war during the War of 1812. *ADM 103 Prisoners of War, 1755 to 1831* contains these records. The records usually give detailed descriptions with the places of birth and show the ultimate disposal of the prisoners. *British Prisoners of War, c1760–1919*, Research Information Leaflet, contains an overview of all records relating to POWs.

Merchant Marine Records

Merchant seamen worked aboard commercial vessels. The Board of Trade (BT) kept merchant marine records. These records, from 1835 to 1860, are at the PRO and include Irishmen who served on British ships.

Several BT classes contain registers of seamen, records for masters and mates, and muster rolls of the crews. *BT 112 Registrar General of Shipping and Seamen, Register of Seamen, Series II, 1835 to 1844* gives the name, age, and birthplace of seamen. *BT 119 Registrar General of Shipping and*

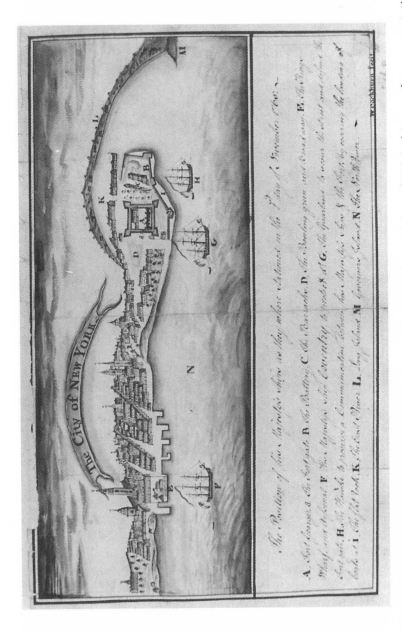

View of the City of New York and Fort St. George showing the position of H.M. ships as they were stationed on November 1, 1765 (MPI 168)

Seamen, Alphabetical Index of Seamen, 1835 to 1844 indexes *BT 112*. *BT 114 Registrar General of Shipping and Seamen, Alphabetical Index to Registers of Seamen's Tickets, 1845 to 1854* indexes the registers of seamen's tickets in *BT 113 Registrar General of Shipping and Seamen, Register of Seamen's Tickets, 1845 to 1854*. Masters and mates certificates of competency are in *BT 122* to *BT 128* and are indexed in *BT 127 Registrar General of Shipping and Seamen's Indexes to Registers of Certificates of Competency and Service, Masters and Mates, Home and Foreign Trade, 1845 to 1894*. *BT 115 Registrar General of Shipping and Seamen, Alphabetical Register of Masters, 1845 to 1854* is also of interest. Muster rolls and crew lists are in *BT 98 Registrar General of Shipping and Seamen, Agreements and Crew Lists, Series 1, 1747 to 1860,* which is arranged by port.

Records for masters, mates, and seamen who served in the British merchant marine during World War I and the interwar period were transferred to the PRO during 1998. Of special interest is *BT 350 Special Alphabetical Index Series (CR 10)* for the period 1915 to 1921 (records for 1915 to 1918 are missing), which are index cards containing personal details, the ships a man served on, and usually a photograph of the individual. Later series of index cards, both for 1921 to 1941, are *BT 348 Central Index, Numerical Series (CR 2)* and *BT 349 Central Index, Alphabetical Series (CR 1)*. An overall index is in *BT 364 Combined Numerical Index*. For more information on this complex subject, see the PRO's web site.

Details of these and other records of seamen and shipping will be found in Public Record Office Reader's Guide no. 20, *Records of Merchant Shipping and Seamen*, by Kelvin Smith, Christopher T. Watts, and Michael J. Watts.

Trinity House Petitions (London: Society of Genealogists, 1987) is a published index to applications for relief from seamen's widows and dependents at the Society of Genealogists in London. Also helpful to North American genealogy researchers tracing merchant marine ancestors in the PRO are *Merchant Seamen: Registers of Service, 1913–1941; Merchant Shipping: Crew Lists and Agreements After 1861;* and *Records of the Registrar General of Shipping and Seamen,* Research Information

Leaflets; and Christopher T. Watts' *My Ancestor Was a Merchant Seaman: How Can I Find Out More About Him?* by Christopher T. Watts and Michael J. Watts (London: Society of Genealogists, 1986). The Family History Library also has microfilm of much of the Board of Trade information for merchant seamen.

Taxation

Tax records are not generally considered to be the first place to begin a search for family history information. They are difficult to identify and use, are often unindexed, and give limited information. An introduction to some of these records can be found in the leaflet *Taxation Records Before 1600*. Numerous types of tax records are in the PRO: apprenticeship records, hearth tax records, land tax assessments, lay subsidies (personal property taxes), poll taxes, and others. Of these, apprenticeship and hearth tax records are highlighted below.

Apprenticeship Records

By law, since 1563 anyone entering a trade had to serve an apprenticeship, and from 1710 to 1811 a central register of apprentices was effectively created for England and Wales by the imposition of a tax assessed on the money a master received for an apprenticeship indenture. The resulting records at the PRO have been indexed by the Society of Genealogists for the period from 1710 to 1774. Also at the Society of Genealogists are seventeen volumes containing miscellaneous original apprenticeship indentures dating from 1641 to 1888. Known as Crisp's Bonds, they list about 18,000 apprentices and have a separate typescript index.

Apprenticeship evidence should also be sought locally. William Brewer Stephens' *Sources for English Local History*, rev. and expanded ed. (Cambridge; New York: Cambridge Univ. Press, 1981) and John West's *Village Records*, rev. ed. (Chichester, Sussex: Phillimore & Co., 1997) discuss local sources. Tax information, including apprenticeship information, continues to be published by local record societies. Jeremy Sumner Wycherley Gibson's *The Hearth Tax, Other Later Stuart Tax Lists, and the Association Oath Rolls,* 2nd ed. (Baltimore: Genealogical Publishing Co., 1996), and Edward Lindsay Carson Mullins' *Texts and Calendars: An Analytical Guide to Serial Publications* and *Texts and Calendars II* survey this literature. While the published literature will be available in large libraries, the Family History Library also has microfilm of some original English tax lists in the PRO, including apprenticeship records.

At the PRO, *IR 1 Board of Stamps: Apprenticeship Books, 1710 to 1811* provides a countrywide indexed list of working men and women. The Apprenticeship Books record the names, addresses, and trades of the masters, and the names of the apprentices and dates of their indentures. Until 1752 the names of apprentices' parents are given. Indexes of masters and apprentices' names are in class *IR 17 Indexes to Apprenticeship Books, 1710 to 1774.* Other apprenticeship records in the PRO may be found in other department records. *Apprenticeship Records as Sources for Genealogy*, PRO Research Information Leaflet, details apprenticeship records in the War Office, Admiralty, Registrar General of Shipping and Seamen in the Board of Trade, and Poor Law Union classes.

Hearth Tax

Taxes for each fireplace or stove were collected twice a year from 1662 to 1689, generating the largest number of surviving records and thus the most useful tax records from this period. The records give the name of the householder and number of hearths, as well as the names of persons exempt from the tax due to poverty. Original records are at the PRO, arranged by county and date, and are considered more accurate than later transcriptions, also available at the PRO. Some records may also be in county record offices. Returns for some counties have been published for individual years.

E 179 Subsidy Rolls, etc., 1154 to 1702 lists the surviving records for a number of taxes, including hearth taxes. The list for *E 179* is arranged by county. Published finding aids are *Analysis of Hearth Tax Accounts, 1662–1665*, compiled by Cecil Anthony Francis Meekings, List and Index Society, vol. 153 (London: Swift, 1979); *Analysis of Hearth Tax Accounts, 1666–1699*, List and Index Society, vol. 163 (London: Swift, 1980); Jeremy Sumner Wycherley Gibson's *The Hearth Tax, Other Later Stuart Tax Lists, and the Association Oath Rolls*; and "Kent Hearth Tax" on pages 196–214 of *Exchequer K. R. Lay Subsidy Rolls (E. 179) Part II Gloucester-Lincoln*, List and Index Society, vol. 54 (London: Swift, 1970).

Association Oath Rolls, 1696 to 1697

C 213 Chancery: Petty Bag Office: Association Oath Rolls, 1696 to 1697 lists office holders who swore an oath of loyalty to the Crown around 1696. Included are members of Parliament, government officials, military and naval officers, judges and the legal profession, physicians, clergy, gentry in all the counties of England and Wales, heralds, and the like in foreign plantations. The latter includes burgesses assembled at St. James' City, Virginia, the governor and council of New York Province, and the mayor, recorder and commonalty of New York City.

The Class List for *C 213* is published on pages 89–107 of *List of Records of the Chancery, Petty Bag Office to 1842*, List and Index Society, vol. 25 (London: Swift, 1967). The Bernau Index at the Society of Genealogists, London, partially indexes the Association Oath Rolls. The 1696 Oath Rolls are also described and listed by Cliff R. Webb in "The Association Oath Rolls of 1695," *Genealogists' Magazine*, vol. 21 (December 1983), pp. 120–123, and published in part in Wallace Gandy's *The Association Oath Rolls of the British Plantations [New York, Virginia, Etc.] A.D. 1696* (London: 1922, reprinted Baltimore: Clearfield Company, 1994). Jeremy Sumner Wycherley Gibson's *The Hearth Tax, Other Later Stuart Tax Lists, and the Association Oath Rolls*, as mentioned above, is yet another useful source.

The PRO also has other miscellaneous rolls. These are enumerated in *Guide to the Contents of the Public Record Office*, vol. I, Legal Records, Etc., pp. 39–41.

Maps

Map research at the PRO is no different from research in any government archive. Genealogists must think of which government department or court of law, during the normal course of business, might have created a record or map of interest. Because of this, identifying maps at the PRO is very different from identifying them in a map library. At the PRO, there is rarely an indication in Class Lists that maps are present in documents, and many thousands of maps remain undiscovered and uncatalogued. Although the PRO's huge map collection numbers in the millions and is international in scope, it is not a place of deposit for published Ordnance Survey maps, which are in the British Library. But for North Americans who have successfully bridged the Atlantic and are searching for documentation on their ancestors in England, the PRO map collection is of great importance.

Despite the lack of universal coverage of bibliographic tools, important finding aids for maps do exist. *Maps and Plans in the Public Record Office*, vol. 2, *America and West Indies* (London: HMSO, 1974) is the principal printed catalogue and is likely to be available in large libraries in North America, certainly those with map collections. While this book catalogue is important to North American genealogical researchers, it describes only a tiny fraction of the maps in the PRO. Maps in the Colonial Office **CO 700** and Foreign Office **FO 925** accumulations, thought to be duplicated in the holdings of the British Library, were excluded from the book catalogue.

In light of these challenges to access, it is wise to consult with the Map Room staff. At the PRO Map and Large Document Room there is a Supplementary Card Catalogue, arranged by place, which updates the published catalogue. The card index contains a name index to draughtsmen, survey-

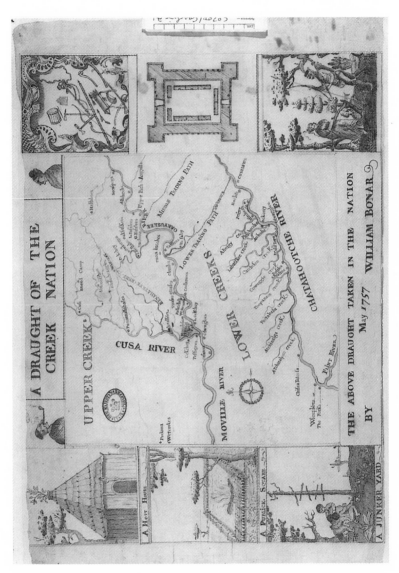

A draft of the Creek nation, 1757 (CO 700/Carolina/21)

ors, cartographers, and the like. Another catalogue includes subjects like plans of gardens, architectural drawings, portraits, and plans and pictures of ships. Augmenting the Map Supplementary Card Catalogue is a Maps and Plans Summary Catalogue, arranged geographically. The volume for North and South America will be of primary interest to North American genealogists. There is also a parallel three-volume subject index.

While the Class Lists are always essential for accessing all classes of records at the PRO, they are especially important for those classes consisting only of maps. ***CO 700 Colonial Office and Predecessors: Maps and Plans: Series I, 1595 to 1927*** consists of maps of colonial North America and contains illustrations of boundaries, towns, lands, and fortifications. *Catalogue of the Maps, Plans and Charts in the Library of the Colonial Office* (London: Colonial Office or HMSO, 1910), reprinted by the List and Index Society in its *Catalogue of Colonial Maps (C 700)*, List and Index Society, vol. 203 (London: Swift, 1984), together with the catalogues previously cited, describes the contents of this record class.

Essential guides to map research at the PRO are Geraldine Beech's "Maps for Genealogy and Local History," *Genealogists' Magazine*, vol. 22 (June 1987), pp. 197–203; William Foot's *Maps for Family History: A Guide to the Records of the Tithe, Valuation Office, and National Farm Surveys of England and Wales, 1936–1943*; *Maps and Plans: Foreign, Colonial and Dominions* and *Maps in the Public Record Office*, PRO Research Information Leaflets.

In North America, the National Archives of Canada has a significant collection of PRO maps and documents ranging from transcripts and photostats to microfilm. The Library of Congress' Geography and Map Division maintains an unsurpassed collection of international maps and cartography. The Family History Library in Salt Lake City has a small collection of Canadian maps and atlases.

Parliamentary Papers

Parliamentary or Sessional Papers are of potential use to genealogists. These papers contain the information needed by Parliament to conduct its business. They include the official sets of bills of the House of Commons and the House of Lords, reports of Select Committees, Command Papers written by royal commissions or government departments, and other reports. While this discussion is devoted primarily to the House of Commons Parliamentary Papers, parallel publications and indexes also exist for the House of Lords. Substantial overlap exists between the publications of the two Houses. To learn more about the House of Lords Parliamentary Papers, see Maurice Francis Bond's *Guide to the Records of Parliament* (London: HMSO, 1971).

There are four major sets of Parliamentary Papers: the official ones published in London by HMSO; Chadwyck-Healey's microfiche set of the House of Commons Parliamentary Papers from 1801 to 1900; the Irish University's 1,000-volume, nineteenth-century reprint set, thought to include about 17 percent of all Parliamentary Papers; and the Scholarly Resources reprint set covering the years 1715 to 1800. Indexes are listed below.

Parliamentary Papers may contain information on North American emigration and land commissions, conditions aboard emigrant ships, slavery, apprenticeships, poor laws, and other topics. Terry Coleman's *Going to America: A History of Emigrants from Great Britain and Ireland to America in the Mid-Nineteenth Century* (Baltimore: Genealogical Publishing Co., 1987) cites references to Parliamentary Papers, including colonization from Ireland, emigrant ships, and reports of the Colonial Land and Emigration Commissioners. Genealogists should also consult Maurice Francis Bond's *The Records of Parliament, A Guide for Genealogists and Local Historians* (Canterbury: Phillimore & Co., 1964); and Percy Ford's *A Guide to Parliamentary Papers, What They Are, How to Find Them, How to Use Them*, 3rd ed. (Totowa, NJ: Rowman and Littlefield, 1972).

Important indexes are the official consolidated indexes to the Parliamentary Papers for 1801 to 1949 in the *General Al-*

phabetical Index to the Bills, Reports, Estimates, Accounts and Papers Printed by Order of the House of Commons and to the Papers Presented by Command, 1801–1948–49, 4 vols. (London: HMSO, 1853–1960); and Luke G. Hansard's *Catalogue of Parliamentary Reports and a Breviate of Their Contents, 1696–1834*, reprinted with an introduction by Percy and Grace Ford (Shannon: Irish University Press, 1969).

Canadian material published in the Parliamentary Papers, vol. 58, pt. 4 (London: The House of Commons, 1847) is indexed in *Indexes to Reports of Commissioners, 1812–1840, Colonies* and *Indexes to Reports of Commissioners, 1828–1847, Emigration*.

Peter Cockton's *Subject Catalogue of the House of Commons Parliamentary Papers, 1801–1900*, 5 vols. (Cambridge, England; Alexandria, VA: Chadwyck-Healey, 1988), indexes the official publications and includes references to Chadwyck-Healey's Parliamentary Papers series on microfiche.

Other Parliamentary Papers indexes from the Irish University Press are the Irish University Press' *Catalogue of British Parliamentary Papers in the Irish University Press 1000-Volume Series and Area Studies Series 1801–1900* (Dublin: Irish University Press, 1977); the Irish University Press' *Checklist of British Parliamentary Papers in the Irish University Press 1000-Volume Series, 1801–1899* (Shannon: Irish University Press, 1972); the *Irish University Press Series of British Parliamentary Papers, General Index*, 8 vols. (Shannon: Irish University Press, 1968); and Percy Ford's *Select List of British Parliamentary Papers, 1833–1899*, by Percy and Grace Ford, rev. ed. (Shannon: Irish University Press, 1969).

Other useful indexes to the Parliamentary Papers are the *House of Commons Sessional Papers of the Eighteenth Century*, edited by Sheila Lambert, 2 vols. (Wilmington, DE: Scholarly Resources, 1975); and the *List of House of Commons Sessional Papers, 1701–1750*, edited by Sheila Lambert, List and Index Society Special Series, vol. 1 (London: Swift, 1968).

Before 1801, Sessional Papers not printed separately were printed in the House of Commons *Journal*. To identify this body of eighteenth-century Parliamentary Papers, see David Menhennet's *The Journal of the House of Commons: A Bibliographi-*

cal and Historical Guide, House of Commons Library Document no. 7 (London: HMSO, 1971), and *Proceedings and Debates of the British Parliaments Respecting North America,* edited by Leo Francis Stock, 4 vols. (Washington, DC: The Carnegie Institution, 1924–1937). Sheila Lambert's comprehensive indexes to the eighteenth-century Parliamentary Papers, cited above, also index the *Journal.*

The PRO's Parliamentary Papers collection is available on microfiche in its Microfilm Room; there's a subject index on CD-ROM. Parliamentary Papers and their indexes, both in paper and microform, are widely available in North American libraries.

Court Records

The Public Record Office also has a great variety of court records. Court records are usually consulted after other records have been investigated. They seldom provide birth, marriage, or death information, but may provide details about occupation, personal appearance, family relationships, and places of residence. However, because they are difficult to identify and use, are usually not indexed, are hard to read, and include unfamiliar legal terms, they are only briefly discussed here.

There are many English courts. The Chancery Court and Court of Exchequer generally relate to wealthier people and can be a source of information about land, property rights, inheritance, debts, trusts, frauds, and lawsuits between individuals. Some cases may mention connections with North America, especially where they deal with shipping and transportation issues. Help in using some of these court records is found in Michelle Cave's *Law and Society: An Introduction to Sources for Criminal and Legal History from 1800;* Henry Horwitz's *A Guide to Chancery Equity Records and Proceedings 1600–1800,* 2nd ed., Public Record Office Handbooks no. 27 (Kew: PRO Publications, 1998); *Chancery Proceedings (Equity Suits)* and *Equity Proceedings in the Court of Exchequer,* PRO Research Information Leaflets; and the PRO's guidebooks to genealogical research at the PRO. The British Record Society's Index Library Series and the PRO Lists and Indexes Series have both published a number of finding aids for Chancery records. To help identify these references, see Edward Lindsay Carson Mullins' *Texts and Calendars: An Analytical Guide to Serial Publications,* and his *Texts and Calendars II: An Analytical Guide to Serial Publications 1957–1982.* The Family History Library has microfilm copies of some PRO court records.

Other English courts are the Assize Court, which dealt with serious criminal cases from the thirteenth century to 1971; the Court of Quarter Sessions, which dealt with a variety of issues, including crime, land, licensing, denization oaths, militia, taxes, and religion; the Manorial Court, which regulated relations between the manorial lord, his officers, and village residents; and the Ecclesiastical Courts, which regulated religious affairs. Of these, only the Assize Court records are at the PRO.

The PRO also has records for the High Court of Admiralty, which initially concerned cases of piracy and spoils but gradually took on all cases involving piracy, privateering, and ships and merchandise on the high seas or overseas. Prior to the sixteenth century much of this business was handled in the Chancery Court. Included in the jurisdiction of the Admiralty Court is the Prize Court, which decided all cases involving prizes taken in time of war, including American ships captured during the American Revolution and the War of 1812.

Appendix A:
Local Record Offices
of England and Wales

A selected list of city and county record offices, current as of 2000, appears below. In some cases published guides to research in the record offices are available and cited; these are revised periodically, so you should check for the most recent editions. For a comprehensive list of British record repositories, see *Record Repositories in Great Britain*, Jeremy Sumner Wycherley Gibson's *Record Offices: How to Find Them*, 8th ed., and other sources cited earlier. When corresponding with record repositories in England and Wales, it is best to add the name of the country to the end of the address and send by air mail. The phone numbers given below are for phoning in England.[4] For direct dialing from the U.S. and Canada, drop the 0 in front of the number, dial 011-44, then the rest of the phone number.

Most record offices now have e-mail addresses and web sites. They have not been included below, but a list of them can be found via ARCHON, which can be accessed through the web site of the Royal Commission on Historical Manuscripts (**http://www.hmc.gov.uk/**).

Many record offices are now part of the County Archives Research Network (CARN), where a reader's ticket obtained at one record office is valid for admission to others. You will need to provide a passport-sized photograph before being issued with a CARN reader's ticket. CARN members are indicated in the following list by the † symbol. A few record offices—Devon, Gloucestershire, Hertfordshire, and

---

[4] City codes for some English cities have changed; every effort has been made to obtain the most recent information.

Lincolnshire—have a small daily charge for using the reading rooms.

Research space in many county and local record offices is very restricted. It is a good idea to telephone a few days in advance of your visit to discuss your research plan and reserve a seat. Many record offices now offer a research service where, for a reasonable fee, enquirers can have research undertaken.

England

BEDFORDSHIRE
Bedfordshire & Luton Archives & Record Office
County Hall, Cauldwell Street
Bedford MK42 9AP
Tel 01234-228833/363222
Fax 01234-228854

BERKSHIRE
Berkshire Record Office†
(The Record Office will be moving to a new address in central Reading during 2000.)
Shinfield Park
Reading RG2 9XD
Tel 0118-901-5132
Fax 0118-901-5131

BRISTOL
Bristol Record Office
'B' Bond Warehouse, Smeaton Road
Bristol BS1 6XN
Tel 0117-922-5692
Fax 0117-922-4236

BUCKINGHAMSHIRE
Buckinghamshire Record Office†
County Hall
Aylesbury HP20 1UU
Tel 01296-382587
Fax 01296-382274

CAMBRIDGESHIRE
Cambridgeshire County Record Office, Cambridge†
Shire Hall
Cambridge CB3 0AP
Tel 01223-717281
Fax 01223-717201
Cambridgeshire County Record Office, Huntingdon†
Grammar School Walk
Huntingdon PE18 6LF
Tel 01480-375842
Fax 01480-459563

CHESHIRE
Cheshire Record Office†
Duke Street
Chester CH1 1RL
Tel 01244-602574
Fax 01244-603812
Guide to the Cheshire Record Office, by Caroline M. Wil-

liams. Chester: Cheshire County Council Libraries, Arts and Archives, 1991, reprinted 1994.

Chester City Record Office†
Town Hall
Chester CH1 2HJ
Tel 01244-402110
Fax 01244-312243

CORNWALL
Cornwall Record Office†
County Hall
Truro TR1 3AY
Tel 01872-273698/323127
Fax 01872-270340
Sources for Cornish Family History, by the Cornwall Record Office, 2nd ed. Truro: The Office, 1995.

CUMBRIA
Cumbria Record Office, Barrow†
140 Duke Street
Barrow-in-Furness LA14 1XW
Tel 01229-894363
Fax 01229-894371
Cumbria Record Office, Carlisle†
The Castle
Carlisle CA3 8UR
Tel 01228-607285
Fax 01228-607299
Cumbria Record Office, Kendal†
County Offices
Kendal LA9 4RQ
Tel 01539-773540
Fax 01539-773439

DERBYSHIRE
Derbyshire Record Office
New Street
Matlock DE4 3AG
Tel 01629-585347
Fax 01629-57611
Derbyshire Record Office Guide, 2nd ed. Matlock: Derbyshire Record Office, 1994.

DEVON
Devon Record Office†
Castle Street
Exeter EX4 3PU
Tel 01392-384253
Fax 01392-384256
Admission fee charged
North Devon Record Office†
North Devon Library and Record Office
Tuly Street
Barnstaple EX31 1EL
Tel 01271-388607
Fax 01271-388608
Admission fee charged
Plymouth and West Devon Record Office†
Unit 3, Clare Place, Coxside
Plymouth PL4 0JW
Tel 01752-385940
Fax 01752-223939
Admission fee charged

DORSET
Dorset Record Office
Bridport Road
Dorchester DT1 1RP
Tel 01305-250550
Fax 01305-257184

DURHAM
Durham County Record Office
County Hall
Durham DH1 5UL
Tel 0191-383-3253
Fax 0191-383-4500
Teesside Archives†
Exchange House, 6 Marton
    Road
Middlesbrough TS1 1DB
Tel 01642-248321

ESSEX
Essex Record Office†
Wharf Road
Chelmsford CM2 6YT
Tel 01245-244644
Fax 01245-244655
    Essex Family History: A
    Genealogists' Guide to the
    Essex Record Office. 4th ed.
    Chelmsford: Essex Record
    Office, 1995.
Colchester and North East
    Branch†
Stanwell House, Stanwell Street
Colchester CO2 7DL
Tel 01206-572099
Fax 01206-574541
Southend-on-Sea Branch†
Central Library
Victoria Avenue
Southend on Sea SS2 6EX
Tel 01702-464278
Fax 01702-464253

GLOUCESTERSHIRE
Bristol Record Office
'B' Bond Warehouse, Smeaton
    Road
Bristol BS1 6XN
Tel 0117-922-5692
Fax 0117-922-4236

Gloucestershire Record Office
Clarence Row, Alvin Street
Gloucester GL1 3DW
Tel 01452-425295
Fax 01452-426378
    Gloucestershire Record Office.
    Handlist of the Contents of the
    Gloucestershire Record Office,
    compiled by Norman William
    Kingsley and revised for the
    3rd edition by David J.H.
    Smith. 3rd ed., Gloucester:
    Gloucestershire County
    Council, 1995 [revised 1998],
    and Gloucestershire Record
    Office. *Handlist of Genealogical*
    Records. Gloucester:
    Gloucestershire County
    Council, new edition 1999.

HAMPSHIRE
Hampshire Record Office†
Sussex Street
Winchester SO23 8TH
Tel 01962-846154
Fax 01962-878681
Portsmouth City Records
    Office†
3 Museum Road
Portsmouth PO1 2LE
Tel 023-9282-7261
Fax 023-9287-5276
Southampton City Archives
    Office
Civic Centre
Southampton SO14 7LY
Tel 023-8083-2251/223855 ext.
    2251
Fax 023-8083-2153

HEREFORDSHIRE
Herefordshire Record Office†
The Old Barracks, Harold Street

Hereford HR1 2QX
Tel 01432-265441
Fax 01432-370248

HERTFORDSHIRE
Hertfordshire Record Office†
County Hall
Hertford SG13 8DE
Tel 01992-555105
Fax 01992-555113

ISLE OF MAN
**Isle of Man Public Record
  Office**
Unit 3, Spring Valley Industrial
  Estate, Braddan
Douglas, IM2 2QR
Tel 01624-613383
Fax 01624-613384

ISLE OF WIGHT
**Isle of Wight County Record
  Office†**
26 Hillside
Newport PO30 2EB
Tel 01983-823820
Fax 01983-823820

KENT
Centre for Kentish Studies†
County Hall
Maidstone ME14 1XQ
Tel 01622-694363
Fax 01622-694379
**Canterbury City and Cathedral
  Archives†**
The Precincts
Canterbury CT1 2EH
Tel 01227-463510
Fax 01227-762897
East Kent Archives Centre
Enterprise Business Park

Honeywood Road, Whitfield
Dover CT16 3EH
Tel 01304-829306
Fax 01304-829306
**Medway Archives and Local
  Studies Centre†**
Civic Centre
Strood, Rochester ME2 4AU
Tel 01634-732714
Fax 01634-297060

LANCASHIRE
Lancashire Record Office†
Bow Lane
Preston PR1 2RE
Tel 01772-263039/254868
Fax 01772-263050
*Lancashire Record Office. Guide
to the Lancashire Record Office,*
by Reginald Sharpe France.
3rd ed. Preston: Lancashire
County Council, 1985, and
1992 Supplement.

LEICESTERSHIRE
Leicestershire Record Office†
Long Street, Wigston Magna
Leicester LE18 2AH
Tel 0116-257-1080
Fax 0116-257-1120

LINCOLNSHIRE
Lincolnshire Archives
St. Rumbold Street
Lincoln LN2 5AB
Tel 01522-525158/526204
Fax 01522-530047
Admission fee charged
**North East Lincolnshire
  Archives**
Town Hall, Town Hall Square
Grimsby DN31 1HX

Tel 01472-323585
Fax 01472-323582

LONDON
**City of Westminster Archives
  Centre**
10 St. Ann's Street
London SW1P 2XR
Tel 020-7641-5180
Fax 020-7641-2179
**Corporation of London
  Records Office**
PO Box 270, Guildhall
London EC2P 2EJ
Tel 020-7332-1251/7606-3030
Fax 020-7332-1119
  *An Introductory Guide to the
  Corporation of London Records
  Office*, by Hugo Deadman
  and Elizabeth Scudder.
  London: Corporation of
  London, 1994.
Guildhall Library
Aldermanbury
London EC2P 2EJ
Tel 020-7332-1862
Fax 020-7600-3384
London Metropolian Archives
40 Northampton Road
London EC1R 0HB
Tel 020-7332-3820
Fax 020-7833-9136
  A General Guide to Holdings. 2
  vols. London: Corporation of
  London, 1993.

MANCHESTER
**Greater Manchester County
  Record Office**
56 Marshall Street, New Cross
Manchester M4 5FU

Tel 61-832-5284
Fax 61-839-3808
  Vincent McKernan. *Guide to
  Greater Manchester County
  Record Office.* Manchester:
  Greater Manchester County
  Record Office, 1993 [revised
  1998].
**Manchester Local Studies Unit
  and Archives**
Central Library
St. Peters Square
Manchester M2 5PD
Tel 0161-234-1980
Fax 0161-234-1927

MERSEYSIDE
**Liverpool Record Office and
  Local History Department**
City Libraries, William Brown
  Street
Liverpool L3 8EW
Tel 0151-225-5417
Fax 0151-207-1342
Merseyside Maritime Museum
Albert Dock
Liverpool L3 4AA
Tel 0151-478-4499
Fax 0151-478-4590
Has collections of material
  relating to emigration from
  Liverpool, but no passenger
  lists.

NORFOLK
Norfolk Record Office†
Gildengate House
Anglia Square
Upper Green Lane
Norwich NR3 1AX
Tel 01603-761349
Fax 01603-761885

NORTHAMPTONSHIRE
Northamptonshire Record
   Office
Wootton Hall Park
Northampton NN4 9BQ
Tel 01604-762129
Fax 01604-767562

NORTHUMBERLAND
Northumberland Record
   Office
Melton Park, North Gosforth
Newcastle upon Tyne NE3 5QX
Tel 0191-236-2680
Fax 0191-217-0905
   Northumberland Records: A
   Guide to the Collections in the
   Northumberland Record Office.[5]
Berwick-upon-Tweed Record
   Office
Council Offices, Wallace Green
Berwick-upon-Tweed TD15
   1ED
Tel 01289-330044 ext. 230
Fax 01289-330540

NOTTINGHAMSHIRE
Nottinghamshire Archives†
County House, Castle Meadow
   Road
Nottingham NG2 1AG
Tel 0115-958-1634/950-4524
Fax 0115-941-3997

OXFORDSHIRE
Oxfordshire Archives†
County Hall, New Road
Oxford OX1 1ND
Tel 01865-815203
Fax 01865-815429

SHROPSHIRE
Shropshire Records and
   Research Centre†
Castle Gates
Shrewsbury SY1 2AQ
Tel 01743-255350
Fax 01743-255355
   Stanley Cedric Clifford.
   Sources of Shropshire Geneal-
   ogy. Shrewsbury: Shropshire
   Family History Society, 1993.

SOMERSET
Bath and North East Somerset
   City Record Office
Guildhall, High Street
Bath BA1 5AW
Tel 01225-477421
Fax 225-477439
Somerset Archive and Record
   Service†
Obridge Road
Taunton TA2 7PU
Tel 01823-278805
Fax 01823-325402

STAFFORDSHIRE
Staffordshire Record Office
County Buildings, Eastgate
   Street
Stafford ST16 2LZ
Tel 01785-278380
Fax 01785-278384
Lichfield Joint Record Office
Lichfield Library, The Friary
Lichfield WS13 6QG
Tel 01543-510720
Fax 01543-411138

---

[5] Forthcoming

SUFFOLK
**Suffolk Record Office, Bury
St. Edmunds Branch†**
77 Raingate Street
Bury St. Edmunds IP33 2AR
Tel 01284-352352
Fax 01284-352355
**Suffolk Record Office,
Ipswich Branch†**
Gatacre Road
Ipswich IP1 2LQ
Tel 01473-584541
Fax 01473-584533
**Suffolk Record Office,
Lowestoft Branch†**
Central Library
Clapham Road South
Lowestoft NR32 1DR
Tel 01502-405357
Fax 01502-405350

SURREY
Surrey History Centre†
130 Goldsworth Road
Woking, GU21 1ND
Tel 01483-594594
Fax 01483-594595

EAST SUSSEX
East Sussex Record Office†
The Maltings, Castle Precincts
Lewes BN7 1YT
Tel 01273-482349
Fax 01273-482341

WEST SUSSEX
West Sussex Record Office
Sherburne House, 3 Orchard
Street
Chichester
Tel 01243-533911
Fax 01243-533959

Address correspondence to
County Hall, Chichester
PO19 1RN

TYNE AND WEAR
**Tyne and Wear Archives
Service**
Blandford House, Blandford
Square
Newcastle upon Tyne NE1 4JA
Tel 0191-232-6789
Fax 0191-230-2614

WARWICKSHIRE
**Warwickshire County Record
Office**
Priory Park, Cape Road
Warwick CV34 4JS
Tel 01926-412735
Fax 01926-412509

WEST MIDLANDS
Birmingham City Archives
Chamberlain Square
Birmingham B3 3HQ
Tel 0121-303-4217
Fax 0121-212-9397
Coventry City Record Office†
Mandela House, Bayley Lane
Coventry CV1 5RG
Tel 024-7683-2418/2414
Fax 024-7683-2421

WILTSHIRE
**Wiltshire and Swindon Record
Office**
County Hall
Trowbridge BA14 8JG
Tel 01225-713136
Fax 01225-713999

WORCESTERSHIRE
Worcestershire Record Office†
Headquarters Branch
County Hall, Spetchley Road
Worcester WR5 2NP
Tel 01905-766350
Fax 01905-766363
Worcestershire Record Office†
St. Helen's Branch
Fish Street
Worcester WR1 2HN
Tel 01905-765922
Fax 01905-765925

YORKSHIRE
**East Riding of Yorkshire
   Archives and Records
   Service**
County Hall
Beverley HU17 9BA
Tel 01482-885007
Fax 01482-885463
Hull City Archives
79 Lowgate
Hull HU1 1HN
Tel 01482-615102
Fax 01482-613091

NORTH YORKSHIRE
**North Yorkshire County
   Record Office**
Malpas Road
Northallerton DL7 8TB
Tel 01609-777585
Fax 01609-777078
Address correspondence to
   County Hall, Northallerton
   DL7 8AF
**York City Archives
   Department**
Art Gallery Building, Exhibi-
   tion Square
York YO1 2EW

Tel 01904-551878
Fax 01904-551877

SOUTH YORKSHIRE
Sheffield Archives
52 Shoreham Street
Sheffield S1 4SP
Tel 0114-273-4756
Fax 0114-273-5009

WEST YORKSHIRE
**West Yorkshire Archive
   Service, Wakefield
   Headquarters**
Registry of Deeds, Newstead
   Road
Wakefield WF1 2DE
Tel 01924-305980
Fax 01924-305983
**West Yorkshire Archive
   Service, Leeds**
Chapeltown Road, Sheepscar
Leeds LS7 3AP
Tel 0113-214-5814
Fax 0113-214-5815

Wales

ANGLESEY
**Anglesey County Record
   Office†**
Shire Hall, Glanhwfa Road
Llangefni LL77 7TW
Tel 01248-752080

CAERNARVONSHIRE
Caenarfon Record Office
County Offices
Caernarfon LL55 1SH
Tel 01286-679095
Fax 01286-679637

CARDIGANSHIRE
**National Library of Wales,
    Department of Manuscripts
    and Records**
Penglais, Aberystwyth SY23
    3BU
Tel 01970-623816
Fax 01970-615709
**Cardiganshire Archives/
    Archifdy Ceredigion†**
County Offices, Marine Terrace
Aberystwyth SY23 2DE
Tel 01970-633697/8
Fax 01970-633663

CARMARTHENSHIRE
**Carmarthenshire Archives
    Service**
County Hall
Carmarthen SA31 1JP
Tel 01267-224184
Fax 01267-224104

DENBIGHSHIRE
Denbighshire Record Office†
46 Clwyd Street
Ruthin LL15 1HP
Tel 01824-703077
Fax 01824-705180

FLINTSHIRE
Flintshire Record Office†
The Old Rectory
Hawarden, Deeside CH5 3NR
Tel 01244-532364
Fax 01244-538344

GLAMORGAN
Glamorgan Record Office
County Hall, Cathays Park
Cardiff CF1 3NE
Tel 029-2078-0282
Fax 029-2078-0284
**West Glamorgan Archive
    Service**
County Hall, Oystermouth
    Road
Swansea SA1 3SN
Tel 01792-636589
Fax 01792-637130

MERIONETHSHIRE
Merioneth Record Office
Cae Panarlag
Dolgellau LL40 2YB
Tel 01341-422341 ext. 4442
Fax 01341-424505

MONMOUTHSHIRE
Gwent County Record Office†
County Hall
Cwmbran NP44 2XH
Tel 01633-644886
Fax 01633-648382

PEMBROKESHIRE
Pembrokeshire Record Office
The Castle
Haverfordwest SA61 2EF
Tel 01437-763707

POWYS
**Powys County Archives
    Office†**
County Hall
Llandrindod Wells LD1 5LG
Tel 597-826088
Fax 597-827162

Appendix B: Useful Addresses

United States

National Archives and Records
    Administration (NARA)
General Reference Branch
7th and Pennsylvania Ave., NW
Washington, DC 20408
Tel 202-501-5400
Web site http://
    www.nara.gov/

Library of Congress
Local History and Genealogy
    Reading Room
Washington, DC 20540-4660
Tel 202-707-5537
Fax 202-707-1957
Web site http://lcweb.loc.gov/
    rr/genealogy[6]

Library of Congress
Manuscript Division
Washington, DC 20540-4680
Tel 202-707-5387
Fax 202-707-6336
Web site http://
    www.lcweb.loc.gov/rr/mss/

Family History Library
35 N. West Temple
Salt Lake City, UT 84150
Tel 801-240-2331
Web site http://
    www.familysearch.org/

Canada

National Archives of Canada
395 Wellington St.
Ottawa, ON K1A ON3
Canada
Tel 613-995-5138
Web site http://
    www.archives.ca/

England

Family Records Centre
1 Myddelton Street
London EC1R 1UW
Tel 011-44-20-7233-9223 (for
    certificate inquiries)

---

[6] For remote access, the Library of Congress provides many resources and services via the Internet. Included on this site is information about public reading rooms and computer centers, traditional and digital collections in numerous formats (text, moving and still image, sound, cartographic, Braille, manuscript, etc.), exhibitions, events, finding aids and bibliographies, photoduplication services, and much more. You may also search the Library of Congress online catalogues.

otherwise
011-44-20-8392-5300
Fax 011-44-20-8392-5307
E-mail service@ons.gov.uk
Web site http://
www.pro.gov.uk/frc
To request civil registration
information by mail, the
address is:
General Register Office
Smedley Hydro
Trafalgar Road
Southport, Merseyside PR8
2HH
England

Principal Registry of the Family
Division
First Avenue House, 44-49
High Holborn
London WC1V 6NP
England
Tel 011-44-20-7936-7000
Fax 011-44-20-7936-6943

Federation of Family History
Societies
The Benson Room
Birmingham and Midland
Institute
Margaret Street
Birmingham, B3 3BS
England
Fax 011-441-21-233-4946
Web site http://
www.ffhs.org.uk/

Public Record Office
Ruskin Avenue
Kew, Richmond, Surrey, TW9
4DU

England
Tel 011-44-20-8392-5200
Fax 011-44-20-8878-8905
Web site http://
www.pro.gov.uk/

Royal Commission on
Historical Manuscripts
Quality House, Quality Court,
Chancery Lane
London WC2A 1HP
Tel 011-44-20-7242-1198
Fax 011-44-20-7831-3550
E-mail nra@hmc.gov.uk
Web site: http://
www.hmc.gov.uk/

Society of Genealogists
14 Charterhouse Buildings
Goswell Road
London, EC1M 7BA
England
Tel 011-44-20-7251-8799
Web site http://
www.sog.org.uk/

The Institute of Heraldic and
Genealogical Studies
82 Northgate
Canterbury
Kent CT1 1BA
England
Tel 011-441-227-768664
Fax 011-441-227-765617
E-mail ihgs@dial.pipex.com
Web site http://
www.ihgs.ac.uk/

Ireland

National Archives
Bishop Street
Dublin 8
Ireland
Tel 011-353-1407-2300
Fax 011-353-1407-2333
Web site http://
    www.kst.dit.ie/nat-arch

General Register Office
Joyce House
8–11 Lombard Street East
Dublin 2
Ireland
Tel 011-353-167-11000
Web site http://
    home.eznet.net/~kinsella/
    genealogy/research/gro.htm

Northern Ireland

Public Record Office of
    Northern Ireland
66 Balmoral Avenue
Belfast BT9 6NY
Northern Ireland
Tel 011-44-28-9025-1318
Fax 011-44-28-9025-5999
E-mail proni@doeni.gov.uk
Web site http://
    proni.nics.gov.uk/

General Register Office
Oxford House
49–55 Chichester Street
Belfast VT1 4HL
Northern Ireland
Tel 011-44-28-9025-2021
Fax 011-44-28-9025-2044
Web site http://
    www.nics.gov.uk/nisra/gro/

Scotland

National Archives of Scotland
HM General Register House
Edinburgh EH1 3YY
Scotland
Tel 011-441-31-535-1314
Fax 011-441-31-557-9569
E-mail research@nas.gov.uk

General Register Office
New Register House
Edinburgh EH1 3YT
Scotland
Tel 011-441-31-334-0380
Fax 011-441-31-314-4400
E-mail nrh.gros@gtnet.gov.uk
Web site http://
    www.open.gov.uk/gros/
    groshome.htm

Appendix C:
Historical County Boundaries

ENGLAND AND WALES

Boundaries Before 1974

SCOTLAND

Northumberland

Cumberland

Durham

Westmorland

Isle of Man

N. Riding

IRISH SEA

Yorkshire

E. Riding

Anglesey

Flintshire

Lancashire

W. Riding

Caernarvonshire

Denbighshire

Cheshire

Derbyshire

Nottinghamshire

Lincolnshire

Merionethshire

Montgomeryshire

Staffordshire

WALES

Shropshire (Salop)

Leicestershire

Rutland

Norfolk

Radnorshire

Cardiganshire

Worcester

Warwickshire

Northamptonshire

Huntingdonshire

Cambridgeshire

Pembrokeshire

Carmarthenshire

Breconshire

Herefordshire

Bedfordshire

Suffolk

Glamorganshire

Monmouth

Gloucestershire

Oxford (Oxon)

Buckinghamshire

Hertfordshire

Essex

Middlesex

London

Berkshire

Wiltshire

Somersetshire

Hampshire (Southhampton)

Surrey

Kent

Devonshire

Dorsetshire

Sussex

Cornwall

Isle of Wight

ENGLISH CHANNEL

Appendix D: Worksheet for Getting Ready

The following worksheet will help in getting records organized before undertaking emigration research using PRO records. The worksheet may be freely copied for personal use without copyright restriction.

Emigration Worksheet

Emigrant's name	
Information About the Emigrant in England or Wales	
Age or date of birth or christening	
Marriage date or other evidence of presence in England or Wales	
County or parish where emigrant lived	
Date emigrant left for North America	
Port from which emigrant left	
Name of ship on which emigrant departed	
Names of persons with whom they emigrated	
Information About the Emigrant in North America	
Date of arrival in North America	
Port of arrival	
Names of place(s) emigrant lived in North America	
Events and dates of emigrant's life in North America (e.g., marriage, birth of children, will, etc.)	
Date and place of death	

Appendix E:
Local Government Records

In Britain, the relationship between the central and local government has varied over the years, and though the clear trend in recent years is toward centralization, the amount of power devolved from the sovereign or from Parliament to local authorities has waxed and waned.

Because of this relationship, local government records may be found in a variety of places. There is much material on local matters in the Public Record Office, varying from medieval charters to reports on schools in the 1930s, from road building plans to lists of seventeenth-century inns. The vast majority of these records are only of marginal interest to family historians, though they may help you find out more about the locality where your ancestors lived in England. For help in using local records, you should consult Philip Riden's *Record Sources for Local History* (London: B. T. Batsford, 1987). Riden is particularly strong on records in the PRO and offers a good introduction to the somewhat tangled relationship between central and local government in England and Wales.

From Anglo-Saxon times to 1974, England and Wales were divided into 58 counties. This was reorganized to 44 in 1974, and then further changes were made in 1986, 1996, and 1998. For genealogical purposes the pre-1974 counties are the most significant, since they are the ones you are most likely to encounter in family history research. A map showing the pre-1974 counties of England and Wales is shown in Appendix C.

Between the fourteenth century and 1888, counties were run by magistrates or justices of the peace (JPs) appointed by the sovereign, who met four times a year or so in quarter sessions to dispense justice and to pass by-laws for the county. The administrative role of JPs was abolished in 1888 when a sys-

117

tem of county councils was established. Quarter sessions continued until 1971, when they were replaced by Crown Courts.

Records of quarter sessions are of great value to family historians, although they can be difficult to use. They include, for example, documents on trials of poachers, murderers, and rioters, as well as certificates for the Hair Powder Tax, declarations of allegiance by Roman Catholics and dissenters, and Bastardy Orders. These records are normally kept at county record offices (see Appendix A). They are described more fully in Jeremy Gibson's *Quarter Sessions Records for Family Historians: A Select List,* 4th ed. (Baltimore: Genealogical Publishing Co., 1995).

Of more importance to the lives of most people were the parish and the borough. By the beginning of the nineteenth century England and Wales were divided into over ten thousand parishes ranging in size from a few hundred yards in the City of London to many tens of square miles in rural Yorkshire. In addition to religious duties, parishes also looked after the poor and elderly, maintained the peace, and repaired local roads. They did this by raising a tax, called rates, on the property of wealthy residents. The system of parishes worked well until the Industrial Revolution, when the boom in population, changes in society, and economic depression overwhelmed this form of local government.

During the nineteenth century parishes gradually lost their non-ecclesiastical powers to a variety of new agencies. The most important of these were the poor law unions, established in 1834 to look after the poor. Responsibility for the registration of births, marriages, and deaths was transferred in 1837 to the General Register Office.

The records of most parishes are found in county record offices. The great variety of these records, from lists of paupers to tithe payments, is described in William Edward Tate's *The Parish Chest: A Study of the Records of Parochial Administration in England,* 3rd ed. (Chichester, Sussex: Phillimore & Co., 1983). For genealogists the most important records are the parish registers, which recorded christenings, marriages, and burials. The location of these registers together with maps of each county showing each parish is given in *The Phillimore Atlas and Index of Parish Registers*, edited by Cecil R. Humphery-Smith.

Towns and cities had separate administrative arrangements. They were governed by charters issued by the sovereign which outlined the rights the town had and how the borough would be administered. Many, for example, had the right to levy a toll at the town market or send representatives to the House of Commons and to hold a court which dealt with civil and some criminal matters. By the early nineteenth century many boroughs had become badly run and corrupt. During the century smaller boroughs lost their separate rights and were absorbed by the counties. New boroughs were created in towns which had grown as a result of the Industrial Revolution, such as Blackburn and Middlesbrough. Cities were at their most influential during the years before the outbreak of the First World War in 1914.

Many borough records are similar to those created by parishes. The best introduction to borough records is John West's *Town Records* (Chichester, Sussex: Phillimore & Co., 1983). Borough records are normally kept at county record offices. Certain ancient boroughs, including Southampton, Coventry, and Chester, have record offices of their own. Their addresses are given in Appendix A.

Wales was slowly absorbed into England between the thirteenth and sixteenth centuries. Until 1964 it did not have a separate administrative entity. As a result, its records are identical to those of England. If you have Welsh ancestry, consult *Welsh Family History: A Guide to Research*, 2nd ed., edited by John and Sheila Rowlands (Baltimore: Genealogical Publishing Co., 1999), the most comprehensive guide to the subject.

Records relating to Scotland and Northern Ireland are not at the PRO. The reason for this is simple. They have status more akin to American states or Canadian provinces than English counties. Their status is guaranteed by the Act of Union of 1707 and the Government of Ireland Act of 1920, respectively. Scottish records, especially, are very different from those in England. If you have Scottish ancestors you should consult one of the many books on this subject, such as Cecil Sinclair's, *Tracing Your Scottish Ancestors: A Guide to Ancestry Research in the Scottish Record Office*.

The Isle of Man and the Channel Islands of Guernsey and Jersey have an unusual relationship to central government. They have long been semi-independent nations with London controlling only their foreign relations and providing defense. The PRO has virtually no records relating to these islands.

Appendix F: Glossary

Following is a brief guide to some of the terms you are likely to come across in using records in the Public Record Office. Some common abbreviations and sources of further information are given on page 129.

Aliens — Regrettably, not men from Mars but non-British citizens resident in Great Britain or the colonies. See also *Denization* and *Naturalization.*

American Loyalists — During the Revolutionary War, as many as one-third of Americans remained loyal to the Crown. At the end of the war many fled to Canada or the West Indies. In Upper Canada, now Ontario, they were called United Empire Loyalists. After the war was over, the treaty of peace in 1783 provided for settlement by the United States of claims of those suffering losses in the former colonies because of their allegiance to the Crown. It took up to twenty years for these claims to be paid.

Annuitants — Persons living on their investments, which may include a pension. A surprising number of annuitants turn up in the census.

Association Oath Rolls — In 1695–1696 all persons in England and Wales holding public office had to swear an oath of allegiance to the Crown.

Attestation papers — A form completed by new recruits to the Army and Royal Marines. They are valuable for genealogists because they contain information about the recruit's origin and sometimes family.

Baptists — Religion founded by an English refugee, John Smyth, in Amsterdam in 1609, which believes in adult baptism. Over the years, the Baptist religion has split into various factions. Most registers of the church before 1837 are now at the PRO. Other records are at Regent's Park College, Pusey Street, Oxford.

Birth, marriage, and death registers — Registers recording births, marriages, and deaths. Until civil or government registration was started on July 1, 1837, all persons had to be married, christened, and buried by the Church of England. By the late eighteenth century, however, many people either did not bother to do so, or chose to do so in another church. Parish registers from Church of England parishes are at local record offices. Many nonconformist registers (sometimes called non-parochial registers), including records of Dr. Williams' Library, are at the PRO. After July 1, 1837, the government took over registrations, though it did not become compulsory until 1875. These registers are at the Family Records Centre, 1 Myddleton Street, London EC1R 1UW.

Board of Trade — A British government department responsible for, among other things, encouraging trade and industry and regulating railways and shipping. First set up by Oliver Cromwell in 1655, its prime interests before 1776 were the colonies in North America. These records are now found in the Colonial Office classes. The President of the Board of Trade is still a ministerial office, although the Board itself has long been part of the Department of Trade and Industry.

British Empire — "The empire upon which the sun never sets," as many Victorian propagandists described it, was made up of many separate colonies. Each was semi-autonomous and reported directly to the Board of Trade or, after 1783, to the Colonial Office in London. The colonies settled mainly by white settlers gradually obtained independence, usually called dominion status. Canada was the first in 1867. Almost all British colonies are now fully independent states; the vast majority of these still remain members of the British Commonwealth.

Census — The first English census was taken in 1801, although few returns for individuals survive before 1841. The primary reason for conducting the early censuses was to determine whether Britain was growing or, as many feared, losing population. As the decades passed, many questions have been added. The censuses are closed to public access for one hundred years after they have been taken. The 1901 census will be the next released and will be available on January 1, 2002.

Chancery — The Court of Chancery dealt with cases for which there was no remedy by common law writ. Later, it came to deal with the rights of one person against another, especially in relation to trusts, wills, marriages, business settlements, tithe matters, and mortgages. Established in the reign of Richard II, it was merged into the High Court in 1857. Its work is graphically described in Charles Dickens' *Bleak House.*

Church of England — The state church of England since the time of Henry VIII. Even today the sovereign remains head of the church. Until the mid-nineteenth century it had important administrative powers, such as registering births, marriages, and deaths and proving wills. Also known as the Anglican Church and, in America, as the Episcopalian Church.

Colonial Office — British government department responsible for administering the British Empire, excluding India. Formally established in 1854, although for many years before then it was part of either the Home Office or War Office. Absorbed into the Foreign and Commonwealth Office in 1967.

Congregationalists — Sometimes known as Independents, this sect believed in the control of each church by its congregation. Most registers of the church before 1837 are now at the PRO. In 1972 the Presbyterians and Congregationalists in England and Wales joined together to form the United Reform Church.

Crown — The institution of the monarch from which all governmental power in Britain flows.

Death records — See *Birth, marriage, and death registers.*

Denization — A half-way house to naturalization. It was less expensive than naturalization. This gave the status of a British subject without the full rights of a native born person, such as being able to hold public office or inherit land.

Entry books — These were books into which copies of letters were written before other means of copying were invented during the nineteenth century.

Exchequer — Historically, the King's treasury, although this role had disappeared by the seventeenth century. Thereafter, it was the senior court of common law covering a wide variety of suits, mainly relating to debts, wills, land, mineral rights, and tithe disputes, until absorbed into the Court of Chancery in 1842.

Family Records Centre — The Family Records Centre is a merger of the Registrar General's public reading rooms in St. Catherine's

House (and before then in Somerset House), where registers of vital statistics for England and Wales from 1837 could be consulted, and the census reading rooms, which used to be in the basement of the PRO building in Chancery Lane (and before then in Portugal Street). On the first floor are birth, marriage, adoption, and death records; on the second floor are census records, nonconformist registers, and Prerogative Court of Canterbury wills.

General Register Office — This office was established in 1836 to administer civil registration of births, marriages, and deaths. From 1840 it became responsible for the national census held every ten years. As the Office for National Statistics (ONS), it now also conducts a variety of other surveys.

High Court of the Admiralty — Originally established to deal with cases of piracy and booty, it came to hear all manner of cases relating to the high seas and business abroad. It was merged into the High Court in 1875.

Home Office — The Home Office was established in 1782 to run the internal affairs of England, a function it still performs. It is responsible, among other things, for naturalization and law and order.

Huguenots — French Protestants. The first refugees arrived in Britain during the mid-1500s. In 1685 there was an influx of 40,000 after the revocation of the Edict of Nantes. They tended to concentrate in London (especially in the Spitalfields district), the Cinque Ports in Kent and Sussex, Norwich, Bristol, and the West Country.

Indentured servants — People aged between fifteen and twenty-one who entered into an indenture, or legal agreement, for a period of up to eight years in return for passage to North America. Indentured servants were often treated as little better than slaves.

Inventories — Annex to a will which lists all the possessions belonging to the deceased. They are common until the mid-eighteenth century, but uncommon thereafter. Although often somewhat difficult to read, they offer a fascinating glimpse into the everyday lives of our ancestors.

Letters of administration — Process to dispose of the property of persons who died intestate, that is, without making a will. Usually abbreviated as "admons" in probate records.

Marriage records — See *Birth, marriage, and death registers.*

Methodists — Perhaps the most successful of the eighteenth-century nonconformist sects, Methodism was founded by John Wesley in 1740. Most of the registers of the church before 1837 are now at the PRO. Other records are held at local record offices.

Militia — From Anglo-Saxon times able-bodied men were liable to perform military service for local defense and occasionally further afield. By the eighteenth century the militia on the whole consisted of volunteers. During the nineteenth and twentieth centuries they had a variety of titles, including Volunteers, Yeomanry (volunteer cavalry units), Territorials, and Special Reserve.

Minute books — Books which contained minutes, or records, of decisions made at meetings.

Moravians — Followers of the Bohemian preacher Jan Huss (Moravia is a district in the Czech Republic). A number of settlements were established during the mid-eighteenth century in northern England, some of which still exist. Most registers of the church before 1837 are now at the PRO.

Muster rolls — Musters are regular roll calls of men in a particular unit or ship.

Naturalization — The process by which a person of foreign birth can become a citizen of another country. The majority of foreigners settling in England did not bother to seek naturalization as it was expensive and difficult to obtain. See also *Denization.*

Nonconformists — People who did not conform to the teachings and rites of the Church of England. The term normally applies to members of sects, such as the Baptists, Quakers, and Methodists (see also entries for these sects), which broke away from the established church in the seventeenth and eighteenth centuries. Nonconformity was very regionalized, with particular strengths in the new industrial areas and in East Anglia.

Officers — Navy, Army, and Air Force officers received the sovereign's commission, a splendid looking document normally signed by the monarch of the day. They are easily traced through the Army, Navy, or Air Force Lists published annually.

Ordnance Survey — Since the 1790s the Ordnance Survey has been the official British mapmaker. Their handsome and very accurate maps are valuable aids for genealogists. Reproductions have been made of a number of series of nineteenth-century Ordnance Survey maps. One-inch maps, each roughly covering a county, are available from David and Charles, Newton Abbott, Devon TQ12 4YG. Many more detailed maps of towns and cities have been reproduced by Alan Godfrey, 57–58 Spoor Street, Dunstan, Gateshead, Tyne and Wear NE11 9BD.

Other ranks — The British equivalent of enlisted men. Non-commissioned officers (NCOs) were corporals, sergeants, warrant officers, and their equivalents in the Navy and Royal Air Force. It will help you considerably in your searches if you know what regiment a soldier served with or the ship a sailor served on, since records tend to be organized by regiment or ship. The naval equivalents are ratings, and the air force airmen/women.

Palatines — German refugees from religious persecution, many originally from the Palatinate (Pfalz) area of southwestern Germany. Some settled in England, but many went to the British colonies of North America, especially to Pennsylvania.

Passenger lists — Lists of passengers on board ship, normally compiled by the ship's captain or purser. The PRO has some for the seventeenth and eighteenth centuries, but the main series runs from 1890 to 1960. See the section on Passenger Lists, chapter 4, for more details. Ports in both the United States and Canada may have required passenger lists long before they became a legal requirement for ships arriving in or leaving Britain.

Paupers — Poor people.

Poor law — Regulations relating to the care of the poor. Before 1603 there was in effect no state provision for the poor and the elderly. Between 1603 and 1834, under the old Poor Law, responsibility lay with parishes. The system could not cope with the pressures of the Industrial Revolution, however. The new Poor Law introduced in 1834 established 600 or so Poor Law Unions which were closely regulated by central government. These Unions lasted until 1929. Records created under the new and old Poor Laws are held at local record offices. They contain much of use to genealogists and include, for example, records of people whose passage to North America was paid for by the parish.

Prerogative Court of Canterbury — The Prerogative Court of Canterbury, usually referred to by its initials PCC, was the senior court of the archdiocese of Canterbury as well as of the Church of England as a whole. As a result, many important wills were proved there, especially if they involved property in one or more diocese. During the nineteenth century, larger numbers of wills came to be proved there. The records are at the PRO.

Prerogative Court of York — The Prerogative Court of York (PCY) was the senior court of the archdiocese of York, which roughly covers England north of the river Trent. Records of the PCY are at the Borthwick Institute in York.

Presbyterians — Followers of the doctrines of John Calvin. The church was particularly strong in Scotland. Most registers of the church before 1837 are now at the PRO. In 1972 the Presbyterians and Congregationalists in England and Wales joined together to form the United Reform Church.

Privy Council — Originally the Privy Council consisted of the King's advisors. It was at its most influential in Tudor times, but after the Restoration in 1660 the Council lost most of its powers to other bodies. However, it remains the final court of appeal for many Commonwealth countries. Much of its administrative work is carried out by committees, some of which (notably Education and Board of Trade) have evolved into separate ministries.

Probate records — The records created during the process of proving wills.

Public Record Office — The national archives of the United Kingdom and England and Wales. Sometimes called "the nation's memory," the PRO was established in 1838 to keep British government records for posterity. Four hundred and seventy staff now look after ninety-five miles (155 km.) of records from the Domesday Book of 1086 to recent government reports. Its records, as this guide suggests, are a gold mine for genealogists with British ancestors.

Quakers — Members of the Society of Friends, a sect founded in the 1650s by George Fox. Many early registers are now at the PRO. They kept many detailed records of their own, which are now at Friends House, Euston Road, London NW1 2BJ. Leaflets describing the records are available free from the Librarian at Friends House.

Quarter sessions — The meeting four or so times a year of the county's magistrates to try criminal cases and administer the county's affairs. Records are held at local record offices.

Recusants — People who were Roman Catholics in the years between the 1540s and 1780s when the Roman Catholic church was outlawed. As being a Catholic could be dangerous, the survival of records from this period is very patchy, although there are some records in the PRO. Despite the Reformation, Catholicism remained strong in certain parts of England. Lancashire in particular was a stronghold.

Rolls — Many older PRO documents are called rolls because they consist of parchment or paper stitched together in a long roll. They can be very cumbersome to use.

Roman Catholics — See *Recusants.*

Transportation — As an alternative to the death sentence many criminals were sent to the colonies for a specified number of years by assize courts and quarter sessions. British colonies in the West Indies and Georgia, Maryland, and Virginia were popular destinations during the eighteenth century. The system reached its peak with the settlement of parts of Australia by transported convicts.

Treasury — The Treasury developed as a separate department during the reign of Elizabeth I. For the last four hundred years it has been responsible for the control and management of public revenue and expenditure.

Treasury Solicitor — The Treasury Solicitor acts as legal advisor to many British government departments. The Treasury Solicitor is also responsible for the administration of the estates of people who died intestate.

Wills — A statement or declaration providing for the disposal of property and possessions after death. Before 1900 perhaps only 10 percent of people left wills in England and Wales. Before 1883 married women could not make a will, and their effects automatically passed to their husbands. Until the nineteenth century the administration of wills was regarded as a duty of the Church of England, since wills were regarded as being between the maker of the will (testator) and God. Because of the nature of Church administration, records can be difficult to find. A new state system was established in 1858 and all wills are now proved by the central government and can be inspected at the Principal Registry of the Family Division, First Avenue House, 44–49 High Holborn, London WC1V 6NP.

Some Common Abbreviations

Admon	Letter of administration
Ag Lab	Agricultural laborer
CEB	Census Enumeration Book
FKW	Frame knit worker
GRO	General Register Office
HM	His/Her Majesty's
HMS	His/Her Majesty's Ship
NCO	Non-commissioned officer
OS	Ordnance Survey
PCC	Prerogative Court of Canterbury
RAF	Royal Air Force
RM	Royal Marine
RN	Royal Navy

Further Reading

Much of the information in this glossary was taken from Pauline A. Saul's *The Family Historian's Enquire Within,* 5th ed. (Birmingham: Federation of Family History Societies, 1995). This invaluable book answers most queries relating to British genealogy. Also consulted were Stella Colwell's *Dictionary of Genealogical Sources in the Public Record Office*, John Richardson's *The Local Historian's Encyclopedia,* 2nd ed. (New Barnet, Historical Publications Ltd., 1986), and *Guide to the Contents of the Public Record Office.*

Bibliography

The bibliography gives complete references for works cited in the text. While an attempt has been made to reference the most recent editions, readers should be aware that some works, such as those of Jeremy Gibson and the publications of the Federation of Family History Societies, are regularly updated, and it is worthwhile to see if more recent editions are available.

The Air Force List. London: HMSO, 1918– .

Allen, Robert S. *Loyalist Literature: An Annotated Bibliographic Guide to the Writings on the Loyalists of the American Revolution*. Toronto: Dundurn Press, 1982.

Andrews, Charles McLean. *Guide to the Materials for American History, to 1783, in the Public Record Office of Great Britain*, 2 vols. Washington, DC: Carnegie Institution, 1912–1914.

Antliff, Bruce. *Loyalist Settlements, 1783–1789*. Toronto: Archives of Ontario, 1985.

Archives of Maryland, vols. 1–72, 1883–1972; New ser. vol. 1– , 1990– . Baltimore: Maryland Historical Society and Maryland State Archives.

Army Lists. London: various publishers, 1754– .

Banks, Charles Edward. *Topographical Dictionary of 2885 English Emigrants to New England, 1620–1650*, 3rd ed. Baltimore: Genealogical Publishing Co., 1963.

Barck, Oscar Theodore. *Colonial America*, by Oscar Theodore Barck, Jr. and Hugh Talmage Lefler, 2nd ed. New York: Macmillan, 1968.

Beech, Geraldine. "Maps for Genealogy and Local History," *Genealogists' Magazine*, vol. 22 (June 1987), pp. 197–203.

Bloomfield, Valerie. *Resources for Canadian Studies in Britain with Some Reference to Europe*, 2nd ed. Ottawa: British Association for Canadian Studies, 1983.

Bond, Maurice Francis. *Guide to the Records of Parliament*. London: HMSO, 1971.

Bond, Maurice Francis. *The Records of Parliament, A Guide for Genealogists and Local Historians*. Canterbury: Phillimore & Co., 1964.

Breed, Geoffrey R. *My Ancestors Were Baptists*. London: Society of Genealogists, 1988.

Bunnell, Paul J. *Research Guide to Loyalist Ancestors: A Directory to Archives, Manuscripts, and Published Sources*. Bowie, Maryland: Heritage Books, 1990.

Camp, Anthony J. *Wills and Their Whereabouts*. London: Society of Genealogists, 1974.

Canada. Public Archives. *A Guide to the Documents in the Manuscript Room at the Public Archives of Canada*, by David W. Parker, Publications of the Archives of Canada no. 10. Ottawa: Government Printing Bureau, 1914.

Candler, Allen Daniel. *The Revolutionary Records of the State of Georgia*, 3 vols. Atlanta: The Franklin-Turner Company, 1908.

Canterbury, England. (Diocese) District Probate Registry. *Index of Wills and Administrations Now Preserved in the Probate Registry at Canterbury* . . . . London: The British Record Society, 1920– . Vol. 50 of the British Record Society's Index Library indexes wills and administrations for 1396–1558 and 1640–1650, transcribed and arranged by Henry R. Plomer, 1920; vol. 65 indexes wills and administrations for 1539–1545, edited by C. Harold Ridge, 1940.

Canterbury, England. (Province) Prerogative Court. *Abstracts of Probate Acts in the Prerogative Court of Canterbury, 1630–1655*, edited by John and George Frederick Matthews, 8 vols. London: 1902–1928.

Canterbury, England. (Province) Prerogative Court. *Abstracts of Probates and Sentences in the Prerogative Court of Canterbury, 1620–1624*, edited by John and George Frederick Matthews. London: 1911.

Canterbury, England. (Province) Prerogative Court. *Administrations in the Prerogative Court of Canterbury, 1559–1580*, edited by Reginald Morshead Glencross, 2 vols. Exeter: W. Pollard & Co., 1912–1917.

Canterbury, England. (Province) Prerogative Court. *Prerogative Court of Canterbury, Inventories, Series II: Part I 1702; 1718–1733*, List and Index Society, vol. 85. London: Swift, 1973.

Canterbury, England. (Province) Prerogative Court. *Prerogative Court of Canterbury, Inventories, Series II: Part II 1734–1782, with Index,* List and Index Society, vol. 86. London: Swift, 1973.

Canterbury, England. (Province) Prerogative Court. *Sentences and Complete Index Nominum (Probates and Sentences) for the Years 1630–1639,* edited by John and George Frederick Matthews. London: 1907.

Canterbury, England. (Province) Prerogative Court. *Wills, Sentences and Probate Acts, 1661–1670,* edited by John Harold Morrison. London: J. H. Morrison, 1935.

Cave, Michelle. *Law and Society: An Introduction to Sources for Criminal and Legal History from 1800,* Public Record Office Readers' Guide no. 14. London: PRO Publications, 1996.

Church of England. Province of Canterbury. Prerogative Court. *Index of Wills Proved in the Prerogative Court of Canterbury . . . .* London: The British Record Society, 1893– . Vol. 10 of the British Record Society's Index Library indexes wills for 1383–1558, A–J, compiled by J. Challenor C. Smith, 1893; vol. 11 indexes wills for 1383–1558, K–Z, 1895; vol. 18 indexes wills for 1558–1583, compiled by S. A. Smith and edited by Leland L. Duncan, 1898; vol. 25 indexes wills for 1584–1604, compiled by S. A. Smith and edited by Edward Alexander Fry, 1901; vol. 43 indexes wills for 1605–1619, compiled by Ethel Stokes, 1912; vol. 44 indexes wills for 1620–1629, 1912; vol. 54 indexes wills for 1653–1656, edited by Thomas M. Blagg and Josephine Skeate Moir, 1925; vol. 61 indexes wills for 1657–1660, edited by Thomas M. Blagg, 1936; vol. 67 indexes wills for 1671–1675, edited by John Ainsworth, 1942; vol. 71 indexes wills for 1676–1685, edited by C. Harold Ridge, 1948; vol. 77 indexes wills for 1686–1693, edited by C. Harold Ridge, 1958; and vol. 80 indexes wills for 1694–1700, edited by Marc Fitch, 1960.

Church of England. Province of Canterbury. Prerogative Court. *Index to Administrations in the Prerogative Court of Canterbury . . . .* London: The British Record Society, 1944– . Vol. 68 of the British Record Society's Index Library indexes administrations in the Principal Probate Registry, Somerset House, London, for 1649–1654, edited by John Ainsworth, 1944; vol. 72 indexes administrations for 1655–1660, A–F, edited by C. Harold Ridge, 1949; vol. 74 indexes administrations for 1665–1660–, G–Q, edited by C. Harold Ridge, 1952; vol. 75 indexes administrations for 1655–1660,

R–Z, edited by C. Harold Ridge, 1953; vol. 76 indexes administrations for 1581–1596, edited by C. Harold Ridge, 1954; vol. 83 indexes administrations for 1609–1619, edited by Marc Fitch, 1968; and vol. 100 indexes administrations for 1631–1648, edited by Marc Fitch.

Church of England. Province of Canterbury. Prerogative Court. *An Index to the Wills Proved in the Prerogative Court of Canterbury, 1750–1800*, edited by Anthony J. Camp, 6 vols. London: Society of Genealogists, 1976–1992.

Church of England. Province of Canterbury. Prerogative Court of Canterbury. *Letters of Administration, 1620–1630*, edited by John Harold Morrison. London: J. Morrison, 1935.

Church of England. Province of Canterbury. Prerogative Court. *PCC Filed Exhibits with Inventories (PROB 32), 1662–1720 Index*, List and Index Society, vol. 204. London: Swift, 1984.

Church of England. Province of Canterbury. Prerogative Court. *Principal Probate Registry: Prerogative Court of Canterbury Paper Inventories 1661–c.1725 (PROB 5): List and Index*, List and Index Society, vol. 149. London: Swift, 1978.

Church of Jesus Christ of Latter-day Saints. Family History Library. *Research Outline: Canada*. Salt Lake City: Family History Library, 1993.

Church of Jesus Christ of Latter-day Saints. Family History Library. *Research Outline: England*. Salt Lake City: Family History Library, 1997.

Clifford, Stanley Cedric. *Sources of Shropshire Genealogy*. Shrewsbury: Shropshire Family History Society, 1993.

Cockton, Peter. *Subject Catalogue of the House of Commons Parliamentary Papers, 1801–1900*, 5 vols. Cambridge, England; Alexandria, VA: Chadwyck-Healey, 1988.

Coldham, Peter Wilson. *American Migrations 1765–1799*. Baltimore: Genealogical Publishing Co., 2000.

Coldham, Peter Wilson. *American Wills and Administrations in the Prerogative Court of Canterbury, 1610–1857*. Baltimore: Genealogical Publishing Co., 1989.

Coldham, Peter Wilson. *American Wills Proved in London, 1611–1775.* Baltimore: Genealogical Publishing Co., 1992.

Coldham, Peter Wilson. *The Bristol Registers of Servants Sent to Foreign Plantations, 1654–1686.* Baltimore: Genealogical Publishing Co., 1988.

Coldham, Peter Wilson. *The Complete Book of Emigrants in Bondage, 1614–1775.* Baltimore: Genealogical Publishing Co., 1988, and 1992 Supplement.

Coldham, Peter Wilson. *The Complete Book of Emigrants, 1607–1776,* 4 vols. Baltimore: Genealogical Publishing Co., 1987–1993.

Coldham, Peter Wilson. *Emigrants in Chains: A Social History of Forced Emigration to the Americas of Felons, Destitute Children, Political and Religious Non-Conformists, Vagabonds, Beggars and Other Undesirables, 1607–1776.* Baltimore: Genealogical Publishing Co., 1992.

Cole, Jean A. and John Titford. *Tracing Your Family Tree.* Newbury: Countryside Books, 1997.

Coleman, Terry. *Going to America: A History of Emigrants from Great Britain and Ireland to America in the Mid-Nineteenth Century.* Baltimore: Genealogical Publishing Co., 1987.

The Colonial Records of North Carolina, 2nd series. Vol. 1– , 1963– . Raleigh, NC: Division of Archives and History.

Colonial Records of Pennsylvania, 16 vols. Harrisburg: T. Fenn & Co., 1851–1853.

The Colonial Records of the State of Georgia, 32 vols. Atlanta: The Franklin Printing and Publishing Co., 1904–1989.

Colwell, Stella. *Dictionary of Genealogical Sources in the Public Record Office.* London: Weidenfeld and Nicolson, 1992.

The Commissioned Sea Officers of the Royal Navy, 1660–1815, edited by David Syrett and R. L. DiNardo, 2nd ed. Aldershot, England: Scolar Press; Brookfield, VT: Ashgate Pub. Co., 1994.

Connecticut (Colony). *The Public Records of the Colony of Connecticut 1636–1776,* 15 vols. Hartford, CT: Press of the Case, Lockwood & Brainard Company, 1850–1890.

Connecticut. *The Public Records of the State of Connecticut,* 15 vols. Hartford, CT: Press of the Case, Lockwood & Brainard Company, 1894–1991.

Cory, Kathleen B. *Tracing Your Scottish Ancestry*, 2nd ed. Baltimore: Genealogical Publishing Co., 1997.

Cox, Jane, and Stella Colwell. *Never Been Here Before? A First Time Guide to the Family Records Centre*, Public Record Office Readers' Guide no. 17. Kew: PRO Publications, 1997.

Cox, Jane. *New to Kew?*, Public Record Office Readers' Guide no. 16. Kew: PRO Publications, 1997.

Cox, Jane. *Tracing Your Ancestors in the Public Record Office* [originally published 1981 and written by Jane Cox and Timothy Padfield], 5th edition by Amanda Bevan, Public Record Office Handbooks no. 19. Kew: PRO Publications, 1999.

Cox, Jane. *Wills, Inventories and Death Duties: The Records of the Prerogative Court of Canterbury and the Estate Duty Office, A Provisional Guide*. London: PRO, 1988.

Crowder, Norman K. *British Army Pensioners Abroad, 1772–1899*. Baltimore: Genealogical Publishing Co., 1995.

Dalton, Charles. *English Army Lists and Commission Registers, 1661–1714*, 6 vols. London: Eyre & Spottiswood, 1892–1904.

Dalton, Charles. *George the First's Army, 1714–1727*, 2 vols. London: Eyre & Spottiswood, 1910–1912.

Dalton, Charles. *Irish Army Lists, 1661–1685*, London: 1907.

Dalton, Charles. *The Waterloo Roll Call*, 2nd ed. rev. and enl. London: 1904.

Delaware. Public Archives Commission. *Delaware Archives*, 5 vols. Wilmington DE, 1911–1916.

Derbyshire Record Office Guide, 2nd ed. Matlock: Derbyshire Record Office, 1994.

Dr. Williams' Library. *Nonconformist Congregations in Great Britain: A List of Histories and Other Material in Dr. Williams' Library*. London: Dr. Williams' Trust, 1973.

The Documentary History of the State of New York, by Edmund Bailey O'Callaghan, 4 vols. Albany: Weed, Parsons and Co., Public Printers, 1849–1851.

Documents Relating to the Colonial, Revolutionary, and Post-Revolutionary History of the State of New Jersey, 47 vols. [spine title *New Jersey Archives*]. Trenton, NJ: 1880–1949.

Documents Relative to the Colonial History of the State of New York, edited by Edmund Bailey O'Callaghan, 15 vols. Albany: Weed, Parsons and Company, 1853–1887.

Dwyer, Clifford S. *Index to Series 1 of American Loyalist Claims: 2 Series, AO 12, Series 1, Microform 30 Reels, AO 13, Series 2, Microfilm 145 Reels* . . . . DeFuniak Springs, FL: Ram Pub., 1985.

Dwyer, Clifford S. *Index to Series II of American Loyalists Claims: 2 Series, AO 13, Series 2, Microform 145 Reels, AO 12, Series 1, Microform 30 Reels* . . . . DeFuniak Springs, FL: Ram Pub., 1986.

Ellis, Roger. "Records of the American Loyalists' Claims in the Public Record Office," *Genealogists' Magazine*, vol. 12 (September 1957), pp. 375–378 and ff.

England and Wales. Exchequer. *Analysis of Hearth Tax Accounts, 1662–1665*, compiled by Cecil Anthony Francis Meekings, List and Index Society, vol. 153. London: Swift, 1979.

Essex Family History: A Genealogists' Guide to the Essex Record Office. 3rd ed. Chelmsford: Essex Record Office, 1993.

The Famine Immigrants: List of Irish Immigrants Arriving at the Port of New York 1846–1851, 7 vols. Baltimore: Genealogical Publishing Co., 1983–1986.

Fellows, Jo-Ann. *A Bibliography of Loyalist Source Material in Canada*. Proceedings of the American Antiquarian Society, vol. 82, part 1, 1972, pp. 67–270.

Filby, P. William. *American & British Genealogy & Heraldry: A Selected List of Books*, 3rd ed. Boston: New England Historic Genealogical Society, 1983 and 1987 Supplement.

Filby, P. William. *Passenger and Immigration Lists Bibliography, 1538–1900: Being a Guide to Published Lists of Arrivals in the United States and Canada*, 2nd ed. Detroit: Gale Research Co. 1988.

Filby, P. William. *Passenger and Immigration Lists Index: A Guide to Published Arrival Records of About 500,000 Passengers Who Came to the United States and Canada in the Seventeenth, Eighteenth, and Nineteenth Centuries*, edited by P. William Filby and Mary K. Meyer, 3 vols., 1981, Cumulated Supplements, 1982–1985 and 1986–1990, Annual Supplements 1991– . Detroit: Gale Research Co.

Fitzgerald, E. Keith. *Loyalist Lists: Over 2,000 Loyalist Names and Families from the Haldimand Papers*. Toronto: Ontario Genealogical Society, 1984.

Foot, William. *Maps for Family History: A Guide to the Records of the Tithe, Valuation Office, and National Farm Surveys of England and Wales, 1936–1943*, Public Record Office Readers' Guide no. 9. London: PRO Publications, 1994.

Foot, William. "'That Most Precious Jewel' East Florida 1763–83," *Genealogists' Magazine*, vol. 24 (December 1992), pp. 144–148.

Ford, Percy. *A Guide to Parliamentary Papers, What They Are, How to Find Them, How to Use Them*, 3rd ed. Totowa, NJ: Rowman and Littlefield, 1972.

Ford, Percy. *Select List of British Parliamentary Papers, 1833–1899*, by Percy and Grace Ford, rev. ed. Shannon: Irish University Press, 1969.

Foster, Janet. *British Archives: A Guide to Archive Resources in the United Kingdom*, edited by Janet Foster and Julia Sheppard, 3rd ed. New York: Stockton Press, 1995.

Fowler, Simon and William Spencer. *Army Records for Family Historians*, 2nd ed., Public Record Office Readers' Guide no. 2. Kew: PRO Publications, 1998.

Fowler, Simon, William Spencer, and Stuart Tamblin. *Army Service Records of the First World War*, 2nd ed., Public Record Office Readers' Guide no. 19. Kew: PRO Publications, 1998.

Fowler, Simon, Peter Elliott, Roy Conyers Nesbit, and Christina Goulter. *RAF Records in the PRO*, Public Record Office Readers' Guide no. 8. London: PRO Publications, 1994.

Fraser, Alexander. *United Empire Loyalists: Enquiry Into the Losses and Services in Consequence of Their Loyalty: Evidence in the Canadian Claims*, 2 vols., originally published in 1905 as *Second Report of the Bureau of Archives for the Province of Ontario*. Baltimore: Genealogical Publishing Co., 1994.

Friends House Library Digest Registers of Births, Marriages, and Burials for England and Wales, 17th c.–1837, 32 microfilm reels. London: World Microfilms Publications, 1989.

Gandy, Wallace. *The Association Oath Rolls of the British Plantations [New York, Virginia, Etc.] A.D. 1696 . . . .* London: 1922, reprinted Baltimore: Clearfield Company, 1994.

A General Guide to Holdings. 2 vols. London: Corporation of London, 1993.

Gibson, Jeremy Sumner Wycherley. *Census Returns 1841–1891 in Microform: A Directory to Local Holdings in Great Britain,* 6th ed. Baltimore: Genealogical Publishing Co., 1997.

Gibson, Jeremy Sumner Wycherley. *The Hearth Tax, Other Later Stuart Tax Lists, and the Association Oath Rolls,* 2nd ed. Baltimore: Genealogical Publishing Co., 1996.

Gibson, Jeremy Sumner Wycherley. *Militia Lists and Musters, 1757–1876: A Directory of Holdings in the British Isles,* by Jeremy Gibson and Mervyn Medlycott, 3rd ed. Baltimore: Genealogical Publishing Co., 1994.

Gibson, Jeremy Sumner Wycherley. *Probate Jurisdictions: Where to Look for Wills,* 4th ed. Baltimore: Genealogical Publishing Co., 1997.

Gibson, Jeremy Sumner Wycherley. *Quarter Sessions Records for Family Historians: A Select List,* 4th ed. Baltimore: Genealogical Publishing Co., 1995.

Gibson, Jeremy Sumner Wycherley. *Record Offices: How to Find Them,* compiled by Jeremy Gibson and Pamela Peskett, 8th ed. Baltimore: Genealogical Publishing Co., 1998.

Giuseppi, Montague Spencer. *Naturalizations of Foreign Protestants in the American and West Indian Colonies (Pursuant to Statute 13 George II, c. 7),* originally published in Publications of the Huguenot Society of London, vol. 24, 1921. Baltimore: Genealogical Publishing Co., 1979.

Gloucestershire Record Office. *Handlist of Genealogical Records.* Gloucester: Gloucestershire County Council, 1992.

Gloucestershire Record Office. *Handlist of the Contents of the Gloucestershire Record Office,* compiled by Norman William Kingsley and revised for the 3rd edition by David J.H. Smith. 3rd ed., Gloucester: Gloucestershire County Council, 1995.

Grannum, Guy. *Tracing Your West Indian Ancestors,* Public Record Office Readers' Guide no. 11. London: PRO Publications, 1995.

Great Britain. Admiralty. *The Navy List.* London: HMSO, 1814– .

Great Britain. Air Ministry. *The Air Force List.* London: HMSO, 1918– .

Great Britain. Board of Trade. *Journal of the Commissioners for Trade and Plantations,* 14 vols. London: HMSO, 1920–1938, reprinted by Kraus Reprint, 1969.

Great Britain. Colonial Office. *Catalogue of Colonial Maps (C 700)*, Lists and Index Society, vol. 203. London: Swift, 1984.

Great Britain. Colonial Office. *Documents of the American Revolution, 1770–1783 (Colonial Office Series)*, edited by Kenneth Gordon Davies, 21 vols. Shannon: Irish University Press, 1972–1981.

Great Britain. Colonial Office. Library. *Catalogue of the Maps, Plans and Charts in the Library of the Colonial Office.* London: 1910, reprinted in London by the List and Index Society as *Catalogue of Colonial Maps (C 700)* in vol. 203, 1984.

Great Britain. Court of Chancery. Petty Bag Office. *List of Records of the Chancery, Petty Bag Office to 1842*, List and Index Society, vol. 25. London: Swift, 1967.

Great Britain. Exchequer. *Class List of Records of the Exchequer King's Remembrancer Part II*, List and Index Society, vol. 108. London: Swift, 1974.

Great Britain. Parliament. House of Commons. *General Alphabetical Index to the Bills, Reports, Estimates, Accounts and Papers Printed by Order of the House of Commons and to the Papers Presented by Command, 1801–1948–49*, 4 vols. (General Index to the Accounts and Papers . . . 1801–1852, Indexes to Bills and Reports, 1801–1852 . . . General Index, 1852–1899, and General Index, 1900–1948–49). London: HMSO, 1853–1960.

Great Britain. Parliament. House of Commons. *House of Commons Sessional Papers of the Eighteenth Century*, edited by Sheila Lambert, 2 vols. Wilmington, DE: Scholarly Resources, 1975.

Great Britain. Parliament. House of Commons. *List of House of Commons Sessional Papers, 1701–1750*, edited by Sheila Lambert, List and Index Society Special Series, vol. 1. London: Swift, 1968.

Great Britain. Parliament. *Proceeding and Debates of the British Parliaments Respecting North America*, edited by Leo Francis Stock, 4 vols. Washington, DC: The Carnegie Institution, 1924–1937.

Great Britain. Privy Council. *Acts of the Privy Council of England, Colonial Series.* 6 vols. London: HMSO, 1908–1912, reprinted by Kraus Reprint in 1966.

Great Britain. Procurator-general and Treasury Solicitor's Dept. *Treasury Solicitor and Procurator General, Class List: Part I (TS 1–10; 12; 14–19)*, List and Index Society, vol. 147. London: List and Index Society, 1978.

Great Britain. Public Record Office. *Analysis of Hearth Tax Accounts, 1666–1699,* List and Index Society, vol. 163. London: Swift, 1980.

Great Britain. Public Record Office. *Calendar of State Papers, Colonial Series, America and West Indies, 1574–1739,* 45 vols. London: HMSO, 1860–1994.

Great Britain. Public Record Office. *Calendar of Treasury Books and Papers, 1729–1745, Preserved in Her Majesty's Public Record Office,* 5 vols. London: HMSO, 1897–1903, reprinted by Kraus Reprint, 1974.

Great Britain. Public Record Office. *Calendar of Treasury Papers, 1556–1728, Preserved in Her Majesty's Public Record Office,* 6 vols. London: Longmans, Green, Reader, and Dyer, 1868–1889, reprinted by Kraus Reprint, 1974.

Great Britain. Public Record Office. *Guide to the Public Record Office* [A multi-volume, loose-leaf, three-part index.] London: Public Record Office, published annually.

Great Britain. Public Record Office. *Exchequer K. R. Lay Subsidy Rolls (E. 179) Part II Gloucester-Lincoln,* List and Index Society, vol. 54, London: Swift, 1970.

Great Britain. Public Record Office. *Exchequer K. R. Port Books 1701–1798: Part I East Coast: Berwick to Yarmouth,* List and Index Society, vol. 58. London: Swift, 1970.

Great Britain. Public Record Office. *Exchequer K. R. Port Books 1701–1798: Part II South-East, South and South-West Coasts: Ipswich to Barnstaple,* List and Index Society, vol. 66. London: Swift, 1971.

Great Britain. Public Record Office. *Exchequer K. R. Port Books 1701–1798: Part III South-West and West Coasts: Plymouth to Carlisle,* List and Index Society, vol. 80. London: Swift, 1972.

Great Britain. Public Record Office. *General Register Office List of Non-Parochial Registers: Main Series & Society of Friends Series,* List and Index Society, vol. 42. London: Swift, 1969.

Great Britain. Public Record Office. *List of Colonial Office Confidential Print to 1916,* Public Record Office Handbooks no. 8. London: HMSO, 1965.

Great Britain. Public Record Office. *List of Colonial Office Records, Preserved in the Public Record Office,* Lists and Indexes no. 36. London: HMSO, 1911, reprinted by Kraus Reprint, 1963.

Great Britain. Public Record Office. *List of Colonial Office Records,* vol. 3: *America,* Lists and Indexes Supplementary Series no. 16. London: Public Record Office, reprinted by the Kraus-Thomson Organization, Millwood, N.Y., 1976.

Great Britain. Public Record Office. *Lists of the Records of the Treasury, the Paymaster General's Office, the Exchequer and Audit Department and the Board of Trade, to 1837,* Lists and Indexes no. 46. London: HMSO, 1921, reprinted by Kraus Reprint, 1963.

Great Britain. Public Record Office. *Maps and Plans in the Public Record Office,* vol. 2, *America and West Indies.* London: HMSO, 1974.

Great Britain. Public Record Office. *Privy Council Office List of Unbound Papers Preserved in the Public Record Office Part I (Bundles 1– 13),* List and Index Society, vol. 24. London: Swift, 1967.

Great Britain. Public Record Office. *Privy Council Office List of Unbound Papers Preserved in the Public Record Office Part II (Bundles 14–66),* List and Index Society, vol. 35. London: Swift, 1968.

Great Britain. Public Record Office. *Privy Council Office List of Unbound Papers Preserved in the Public Record Office Part III (Bundles 142–3020),* List and Index Society, vol. 36. London: Swift, 1968.

Great Britain. Public Record Office. *Records in the British Public Record Office Relating to South Carolina, 1663–1710,* 5 vols. Atlanta: Printed for the Historical Commission of South Carolina by Foote & Davies Company, 1928–1947.

Great Britain. Public Record Office. *The Records of the Foreign Office 1782–1939,* Public Record Office Handbooks no. 13. London: HMSO, 1969.

Great Britain. Treasury. *Treasury Board Papers (T.1/319–364) Descriptive List and Index Mainly 1745–1755,* List and Index Society, vol. 120. London: Swift, 1975.

Great Britain. Treasury. *Treasury Board Papers (T.1/365–388) Descriptive List and Index Mainly 1756–1758,* List and Index Society, vol. 125. London: Swift, 1976.

Great Britain. War Office. *Soldiers Died in the Great War, 1914-19.* London: HMSO, 1920–1921.

Grenham, John. *Tracing Your Irish Ancestors: The Complete Guide.* 2nd ed. Baltimore: Genealogical Publishing Co., 2000.

Guide to British Naval Papers in North America, compiled for the National Maritime Museum by Roger Morriss with the assistance of Peter Bursey. London; New York: Mansell, 1994.

A Guide to Manuscripts Relating to America in Great Britain and Ireland: A Revision of the Guide Edited in 1961 by B. R. Crick and Miriam Alman, edited by John W. Raimo under the general supervision of Dennis Welland, rev. ed. Westport, CT: Published for the British Association for American Studies by Meckler Books, 1979.

Guide to the Cheshire Record Office, by Caroline M. Williams. Chester: Cheshire Co. Council Libraries, 1991, reprinted 1994.

Hansard, Luke G. *Catalogue of Parliamentary Reports and a Breviate of Their Contents, 1696–1834,* reprinted with introduction by Percy and Grace Ford. Shannon: Irish University Press, 1969.

Hart's Annual Army List, Militia List, & Imperial Yeomanry List . . . . London: J. Murray, 1840–1915.

Hawkings, David T. *Criminal Ancestors: A Guide to Historical Criminal Records in England and Wales.* Stroud, Eng.: Alan Sutton, 1992.

Herber, Mark O. *Ancestral Trails.* Baltimore: Genealogical Publishing Co., 1998.

Hey, David. *The Oxford Companion to Local and Family History.* Oxford; New York: Oxford University Press, 1996.

Hey, David. *The Oxford Guide to Family History.* Oxford; New York: Oxford University Press, 1993.

Higgs, Edward. *A Clearer Sense of the Census,* London: HMSO, 1996.

Holding, Norman H. *World War One Army Ancestry,* 3rd ed. Birmingham: Federation of Family History Societies, 1997.

Horwitz, Henry. *A Guide to Chancery Equity Records and Proceedings 1600–1800.* 2nd ed. Public Record Office Handbooks no. 27. Kew: PRO Publications, 1998.

Hotten, John C. *The Original Lists of Persons of Quality: Emigrants, Religious Exiles, Political Rebels, Serving Men Sold for a Term of Years, Apprentices & Others Who Went from Great Britain to the American Plantations, 1600–1700.* Reprint of the 1874 edition. Baltimore: Genealogical Publishing Co., 1983.

Humphery-Smith, Cecil R. *A Genealogist's Bibliography.* Baltimore: Genealogical Publishing Co., 1985.

Humphery-Smith, Cecil R. "The Nature and Origins of Emigration to America," *Family History*, vol. 5 (April 1968), pp. 163–72.

Indexes to Reports of Commissioners, 1812–1840, Colonies, Parliamentary Papers, vol. 58, pt. 4, London: The House of Commons, 1847.

Indexes to Reports of Commissioners, 1828–1847, Emigration, Parliamentary Papers, vol. 58, pt. 4, London: The House of Commons, 1847.

Inland Revenue Estate Duty Registers and Indexes (IR26, IR27), 1796–1894, List and Index Society, vol. 177. London: Swift, 1981.

An Introductory Guide to the Corporation of London Records Office, by Hugo Deadman and Elizabeth Scudder. London: Corporation of London, 1994.

Irish Genealogy: A Record Finder, edited by Donal F. Begley. Dublin: Heraldic Artists, 1987.

Irish University Press. *Catalogue of British Parliamentary Papers in the Irish University Press 1000-Volume Series and Area Studies Series, 1801–1900*. Dublin: Irish University Press, 1977.

Irish University Press. *Checklist of British Parliamentary Papers in the Irish University Press 1000-Volume Series, 1801–1899*. Shannon: Irish University Press, 1972.

Irish University Press Series of British Parliamentary Papers, General Index, 8 vols. Shannon: Irish University Press, 1968.

Irvine, Sherry. *Your English Ancestry: A Guide for North Americans*. Salt Lake City: Ancestry, 1993.

Irvine, Sherry. *Your Scottish Ancestry: A Guide for North Americans*. Salt Lake City: Ancestry, 1997.

Jurkowski, M. (Maureen). *Lay Taxes in England and Wales, 1188–1699*. Public Record Office Handbooks no. 31. Kew: PRO Publications, 1998.

Kaminkow, Marion J. *Original Lists of Emigrants in Bondage from London to the American Colonies, 1719–1744*. Baltimore: Magna Carta Book Company, 1967.

Kirk, Richard Edward Gent. *Returns of Aliens Resident in London, 1523–1603*. Publications of the Huguenot Society of London, vol. 10 (1900–1908).

Kitzmiller, John Michael. *In Search of the "Forlorn Hope": A Comprehensive Guide to Locating British Regiments and Their Records*, 2 vols. Salt Lake City: Manuscript Pub. Foundation, 1988.

Knittle, Walter Allen. *Early Eighteenth Century Palatine Emigration*, originally published 1937, reprinted Baltimore: Genealogical Publishing Co., 1970.

Lancashire Record Office. *Guide to the Lancashire Record Office*, by Reginald Sharpe France. 3rd ed. Preston: Lancashire County Council, 1985 and 1992 Supplement.

Leary, William. *My Ancestors Were Methodists*, 2nd ed. London: Society of Genealogists, 1990.

Leventhal, Herbert and James E. Mooney. *A Bibliography of Loyalist Source Material in the United States*. Proceedings of the American Antiquarian Society, vol. 85, part 1 (1975), pp. 73–308; vol. 85, part 2 (1975), pp. 405–460; vol. 86, part 2 (1976), pp. 343–390.

A List of Wills, Administrations, Etc. in the Public Record Office, London, England 12th–19th Century. Baltimore: Magna Carta Book Company, 1968.

"Lists of Germans from the Palatinate Who Came to England in 1709," *New York Genealogical and Biographical Record*, vol. 40 (1909); pp. 49–54, 93–100, 160–167, 241–248, and vol. 41 (1910); pp. 10–19.

Lumas, Susan. *Making Use of the Census*, 3rd ed., Public Record Office Readers' Guide no. 1. London: PRO Publications, 1997.

MacWethy, Lou D. *The Book of Names, Especially Relating to the Early Palatines and the First Settlers in the Mohawk Valley*, originally published 1933, reprinted Baltimore: Genealogical Publishing Co., 1969.

Massachusetts (Colony). General Court. House of Representatives. *Journals of the House of Representatives*, 55 vols., 1715–1779. Boston: Massachusetts Historical Society, 1919–1990.

Massachusetts (Colony). *Records of the Governor and Company of the Massachusetts Bay*, 5 vols. in 6. Boston: W. White, Printer to the Commonwealth, 1853–1854.

McKenzie, Donald A. "Upper Canada Naturalization Records (1828–1850)," *Families*, vol. 18 (1979), pp. 103–115; vol. 19 (1980), pp. 36–56.

McKernan, Vincent. *Guide to Greater Manchester County Record Office*. Manchester: Greater Manchester County Record Office, 1993.

Menhennet, David. *The Journal of the House of Commons: A Bibliographical and Historical Guide*, House of Commons Library Document no. 7. London: HMSO, 1971.

Milligan, Edward H. and Malcolm J. Thomas. *My Ancestors Were Quakers*. London: Society of Genealogists, 1983.

Minet, William and Susan. *A Supplement to Dr. W. Shaw's Letters of Denization and Acts of Naturalization*. Publications of the Huguenot Society of London, vol. 35 (1932).

Moulton, Joy Wade. *Genealogical Resources in English Repositories*. Baltimore: Genealogical Publishing Co., 1988 and Supplement.

Mullins, Edward Lindsay Carson. *A Guide to the Historical and Archaeological Publications of Societies in England and Wales, 1901–1933*, compiled for the Institute of Historical Research. London: Athlone Press, 1968.

Mullins, Edward Lindsay Carson. *Texts and Calendars: An Analytical Guide to Serial Publications*. London: Royal Historical Society, 1958.

Mullins, Edward Lindsay Carson. *Texts and Calendars II: An Analytical Guide to Serial Publications, 1957–1982*. London: Royal Historical Society, 1983.

Muster Books and Pay Lists: General Series, Cavalry (WO 12/1-13305), List and Index Society, vol. 210. London: Swift, 1984.

National Archives of Canada. *Tracing Your Ancestors in Canada*, 13th ed., rev. Ottawa: National Archives of Canada, 1998.

The Nation's Memory: A Pictorial Guide to the Public Record Office, edited by Jane Cox. London: HMSO, 1988.

The Navy List. London: HMSO, 1782– .

New England: A Bibliography of Its History, prepared by the Committee for a New England Bibliography, edited by Roger Parks. Hanover, NH: University Press of New England, 1989.

New Hampshire. *Documents and Records Relating to the Province (State and Towns) of New Hampshire, from the Earliest Period of its Settlement . . . 1623–1800*, 40 vols. Manchester NH and elsewhere: 1867–1943 (vol. 23 is *A List of Documents in the Public Record Office in London . . . Relating to the Province of New Hampshire*).

New Plymouth Colony. *Records of the Colony of New Plymouth, in New England*, 12 vols. in 10. Boston: Press of W. White, 1855–1861.

North Carolina. *The State Records of North Carolina*, 30 vols., of which the first 10 volumes are *The Colonial Records of North Carolina*. Raleigh: P. M. Hale, 1886–1907.

Page, William. *Letters of Denization and Naturalization for Aliens in England, 1509–1603*. Publications of the Huguenot Society of London, vol. 8 (1893).

Palgrave-Moore, Patrick T. R. *Understanding the History and Records of Nonconformity*, 2nd ed. Norwich, England: Elvery Dowers, 1989.

Palmer, Gregory. *A Bibliography of Loyalist Source Material in the United States, Canada, and Great Britain*. Westport, CT: Meckler Publishing, 1982.

Palmer, Gregory. *Biographical Sketches of Loyalists of the American Revolution*. Westport, CT: Meckler Publishing, 1984.

Parker, David W. *Guide to the Materials for United States History in Canadian Archives*. Washington, DC: Carnegie Institution, 1913.

Paullin, Charles Oscar. *Guide to the Materials in London Archives for the History of the United States Since 1783*, by Charles O. Paullin and Frederic L. Paxson. Washington, DC: Carnegie Institution, 1914.

Pennsylvania Archives, 120 vols., published in nine series. Philadelphia and Harrisburg: J. Severns & Co., 1852–1935.

The Phillimore Atlas and Index of Parish Registers, edited by Cecil R. Humphery-Smith. New ed. Chichester, Sussex: Phillimore & Co., 1995.

Prerogative Court of Canterbury, Parchment Inventories Post 1660 (Prob 4/1-6416), List and Index Society, vol. 221. London: Swift, 1986.

Public Archives of Canada. Manuscript Division. *General Inventory: Manuscripts*, vol. 2, MG11–MG16. Ottawa: 1976.

Public Archives of Canada. Manuscript Division. *Manuscript Division*, by Grace Hyam and Jean-Marie LeBlanc. Ottawa: Public Archives of Canada, 1984.

Public Archives of Canada. *Report on Canadian Archives, 1890, 1894, and 1895*. Ottawa: Printed by Brown Chamberlin, Printer to the Queen's Most Excellent Majesty, 1891, 1895, and 1896.

"The Public Record Office, Chancery Lane and Kew, Some References to Emigration," *Family Tree*, vol. 1, nos. 1,2,3 (Nov.–Dec. 1984), p. 9; (Jan.–Feb. 1985), p. 23; and (March–April 1985), p. 20.

Published American Colonial Records, 166 microfilm reels. New Haven, CT: Research Publications, 1970.

Pugh, Ralph Bernard. *The Records of the Colonial and Dominions Offices*, Public Record Office Handbooks no. 3. London: HMSO, 1964.

Raymond, Stuart A. *English Genealogy: An Introductory Bibliography*, 3rd ed. Birmingham: Federation of Family History Societies, 1996.

Record Repositories in Great Britain, edited by Ian Mortimer, 10th ed. Co-published with the Royal Commission on Historical Manuscripts. London: Public Record Office Publications, 1997.

Records of the Colonial Office, Dominion Office, Commonwealth Relations Office, and Commonwealth Office, edited by Anne Thurston, vol. 1 of *Sources for Colonial Studies in the PRO* and Series C, vol. 1, *British Documents on the End of the Empire*. London: HMSO, 1995.

Reid, Judith Prowse. *Family Ties in England, Scotland, Wales, Ireland: Sources for Genealogical Research*. Washington, DC: Library of Congress, 1998.

Rhode Island (Colony). *Records of the Colony of Rhode Island and Providence Plantations in New England* [spine title *Colonial Records of Rhode Island, 1636–1792*], 10 vols. Providence: A. C. Greene and Brothers, State Printers, 1856–1865.

Richardson, John. *The Local Historian's Encyclopedia*, 2nd ed. New Barnet, Hertfordshire: Historical Publications Ltd., 1986.

Riden, Philip. *Record Sources for Local History*. London: B. T. Batsford, 1987.

Rodger, N. A. M. *Naval Records for Genealogists*, 2nd ed., Public Record Office Handbooks no. 22. London: HMSO, 1998.

Roper, Michael. *Records of the War Office and Related Departments, 1660–1964*. Public Record Office Handbooks no. 29. London: PRO Publications, 1998.

Sabine, Lorenzo. *Biographical Sketches of Loyalists of the American Revolution, with an Historical Essay*, 2 vols. Boston: Little, Brown, and Company, 1864.

Saul, Pauline A. *The Family Historian's Enquire Within,* 5th ed. Birmingham: Federation of Family History Societies, 1995.

Savage, James. *A Genealogical Dictionary of the First Settlers of New England,* 4 vols. Originally published 1860–62, reprinted Baltimore: Genealogical Publishing Co., 1965.

Scott, Miriam. *Prerogative Court of Canterbury Wills and Other Probate Records,* Public Record Office Readers' Guide no. 15, Kew: PRO Publications, 1997.

Shaw, William A. *Letters of Denization and Acts of Naturalization for Aliens in England and Ireland, 1603–1700.* Publications of the Huguenot Society of London, vol. 18 (1911).

Shaw, William A. *Letters of Denization and Acts of Naturalization for Aliens in England and Ireland, 1701–1800.* Publications of the Huguenot Society of London, vol. 27 (1923).

Shorney, David. *Protestant Nonconformity and Roman Catholicism,* Public Record Office Readers' Guide no. 13. London: PRO Publications, 1997.

Siebert, Wilbur Henry. *Loyalists in East Florida, 1774 to 1785; the Most Important Documents Pertaining Thereto, Edited with an Accompanying Narrative by Wilbur Henry Siebert. With a New Introd. and Pref. by George Athan Billias.* Boston, Gregg Press, 1972, originally published in 1929 in Deland, FL by The Florida State Historical Society.

Silverthorne, Elizabeth. *London Local Archives: A Directory of Local Authority Record Offices and Libraries,* 3rd ed. London: Guildhall Library and Greater London Archives Network, 1994.

Sinclair, Cecil. *Tracing Your Scottish Ancestors: A Guide to Ancestry Research in the Scottish Record Office,* rev. ed. Edinburgh: HMSO, 1997.

Smith, Kelvin, Christopher T. Watts, and, Michael J. Watts. *Records of Merchant Seamen and Shipping,* Public Record Office Readers' Guide no. 20. Kew: PRO Publications, 1998.

Sources for Cornish Family History, by the Cornwall Record Office, 2nd ed. Truro: The Office, 1995.

South Carolina (Colony). Assembly. *Colonial Records of South Carolina: Journals of the Commons House of Assembly,* 14 vols. Columbia: Historical Commission of South Carolina, 1951–1989.

Spencer, William. *Records of the Militia and Volunteer Forces 1758-1945,* Public Record Office Readers' Guide no. 3. Kew: PRO Publications, 1997.

Sperry, Kip. *New England Genealogical Research: A Guide to Sources.* Bowie, MD: Heritage Books, 1988.

Steel, Donald J. and Edgar Roy Samuel. *Sources for Roman Catholic and Jewish Genealogy and Family History,* National Index of Parish Registers, vol. 3. London: Published for the Society of Genealogists by Phillimore & Co., 1974.

Steel, Donald J. *General Sources of Births, Marriages, and Deaths Before 1837,* National Index of Parish Registers, vol. 1. London: Published for the Society of Genealogists by Phillimore & Co., 1968.

Steel, Donald J. *Sources for Nonconformist Genealogy and Family History,* National Index of Parish Registers, vol. 2. London: Published for the Society of Genealogists by Phillimore & Co., 1973.

Stephens, William Brewer. *Sources for English Local History,* rev. and expanded ed. Cambridge; New York: Cambridge University Press, 1981.

Tate, William Edward. *The Parish Chest: A Study of the Records of Parochial Administration in England,* 3rd ed. Chichester, Sussex: Phillimore & Co., 1983.

Tepper, Michael. *American Passenger Arrival Records: A Guide to the Records of Immigrants Arriving at American Ports by Sail and Steam.* Baltimore: Genealogical Publishing Co., 1993.

Thomas, Garth. *Records of the Royal Marines,* Public Record Office Readers' Guide no. 10. London: PRO Publications, 1994.

Trinity House Petitions. London: Society of Genealogists, 1987.

Vermont. *Records of the Governor and Council of the State of Vermont . . . ,* 8 vols. Montpelier, VT: Steam Press of J. & J. M. Poland, 1873–1880.

Vermont. Secretary of State. State Papers of Vermont Series, 21 vols.– . Rutland & Bellows Falls, VT: 1918.

Vermont. *Vermont State Papers: Being a Collection of Records and Documents Connected With the Assumption and Establishment of Government by the People of Vermont.* Middlebury, VT: J. W. Copeland, Printer, 1823.

Virginia. *Calendar of Virginia State Papers and Other Manuscripts Preserved at Richmond*, 11 vols. Richmond: Imprint varies, 1875–1893.

Virginia (Colony) Council. *Legislative Journals of the Council of Colonial Virginia* . . . , 3 vols. Richmond: The Colonial Press, Everett Waddey Co., 1918–1919.

Virginia Committee on Colonial Records. *The British Public Record Office: History, Description, Record Groups, Finding Aids, and Materials for American History with Special References to Virginia*, Virginia Colonial Records Project, Special Report, 25–28. Richmond: The Virginia State Library, 1960.

Virginia Company of London. *The Records of the Virginia Company of London*, 4 vols. Washington, DC: U.S. Government Printing Office, 1906–1935.

Virginia. Council. *Executive Journals of the Council of Colonial Virginia*, 6 vols. Richmond: D. Bottom, Superintendent of Public Printing, 1925–1966.

Virginia. General Assembly. House of Burgesses. *Journals of the House of Burgesses of Virginia*, 13 vols. Richmond: The Colonial Press, Everett Waddey Co., 1905–1915.

War Office Regular Army: Soldiers' Documents 1760–1913 (WO 97), List and Index Society, vol. 201. London: Swift, 1983.

Watts, Christopher T. *My Ancestor Was a Merchant Seaman: How Can I Find Out More About Him?* by Christopher T. Watts and Michael J. Watts. London: Society of Genealogists, 1986.

Watts, Michael J. *My Ancestor Was in the British Army: How Can I Find Out More About Him?* London: Society of Genealogists, 1992.

Webb, Cliff R. "The Association Oath Rolls of 1695," *Genealogists' Magazine*, vol. 21 (December 1983), pp. 120–123.

Welsh Family History: A Guide to Research, 2nd ed., edited by John and Sheila Rowlands. Baltimore: Genealogical Publishing Co., 1999.

West, John. *Town Records*. Chichester, Sussex: Phillimore & Co., 1983.

West, John. *Village Records*, rev. ed. Chichester, Sussex: Phillimore & Co., 1997.

Wilson, Bruce G. *Manuscripts and Government Records in the United Kingdom and Ireland Relating to Canada*. Ottawa: National Archives of Canada, 1992.

Wilson, John. *Guide to the South Humberside Area Archive Office*. Hull: Humberside County Council, 1993.

Yeo, Geoffrey. *The British Overseas: A Guide to Records of Their Births, Baptisms, Marriages, Deaths, and Burials, Available in the United Kingdom*, 2nd ed., Guildhall Library Research Guide 2. London: Guildhall Library, 1988.

General Index

(Note: For place names (states, provinces, etc.) in Canada, the United States, and the West Indies, look under Canada, United States, or West Indies. Types of records have also been grouped together for a better overview of what is available, e.g., Emigration records, Naturalization records, Church records, etc.)

Admiralty (Great Britain) apprenticeship records *see* Apprenticeship records

Africa, vital records for British citizens in 71–72

Agent General for Emigration (Great Britain) 47

Air Force (Great Britain) *see* Military records

Aliens in Great Britain *see* Immigration records, Naturalization records

American Loyalists' Claims Commission *see* Loyalists

Apprenticeship records 88–89, 94
    Admiralty records 89
    Board of Stamps records (1710–1811) 89
    Board of Trade records 89
    Crisp's bonds (indentures, 1641–1888) 88
    finding aid to PRO records 26
    Poor Law Union records 89
    Registrar General of Shipping and Seamen records 27, 89
    War Office records 89

Army (Great Britain) *see* Military records

Asia, vital records for British citizens in 71–72

Association oath rolls (1696–1697) 90–91, 121

Audit Dept. (Great Britain) 58

Baptists *see* Church records

Barbados *see* West Indies

Bernau index to Association oath rolls 90

Births, deaths, and marriages *see* Church records, Vital records

Board of Stamps (Great Britain) apprenticeship records *see* Apprenticeship records

Board of Trade (Great Britain) 41–42, 45, 60, 72, 88–89
    apprenticeship records *see* Apprenticeship records

Bonded servants transported overseas *see* Emigration records

Borough records *see* Local government records

Borthwick Institute of Historical Research (York, England) 73

Bristol *see* Emigration records

British citizens in the United States, vital records (20th cent.) 71–72

Buckinghamshire, persons from, mentioned in the Treasury money books 56

Canada
    emigration, settlement, early residents 42–45, 47, 53, 57, 95
    land grants 44, 51, 53
    Loyalists *see* Loyalists
    maps of colonial North America 93
    militia lists (1837–1843) 82

Irish genealogy
    basic books on how to do 3
    guides to archival sources 6–7, 31
    published sources 4
Isle of Man
    census returns 65
    local records in Public Record Office 120
Jews 60, 69
Kent, persons from, mentioned in Treasury money books 56
Land grants in British North America (Canada, U.S., West Indies) 42, 44, 49, 51, 53
    finding aids to PRO holdings 26
    published guides 51
Library of Congress (Washington, DC) 1, 5, 70, 109
    Geography and Map Div. 93
    Manuscript Div. 43, 58
Lincolnshire 90
List and Index Society 29
Local government records (Great Britain) 117–20
Local history/village sources 88–89
Local record offices, England and Wales 99–108
London, persons from, mentioned in Treasury money books 56
London, Port of—emigrants *see* Emigration records
Loyalists 26, 43, 51, 57–60, 121
    American Loyalists' Claims Commission 58, 60
    East Florida Claims Commission 58–59
    finding aids to PRO holdings 26
    Haldimand papers (lists of Loyalists) 57
    refugees (1780–1835) 59
    United Empire Loyalists 57–60
    vital records 60
Maps 24, 26, 59, 91–93
    colonial North America 93

Marines (Great Britain) *see* Military records
Marriage, birth, and death records *see* Church records, Vital records
Merchant marine (Great Britain) 77, 85, 87–88
Merchant navy *see* Merchant marine (Great Britain)
Methodists *see* Church records
Middlesex, persons from, mentioned in Treasury money books 56
Military pension records *see* Military records
Military records *see also* Militia lists
    Army (Great Britain) 24, 70, 77–81
    finding aids to PRO holdings and basic research 27–28, 77
    military records 77–81
    military registers 70
    Ministry of Defence records 81, 84
    pension records 77
    prisoners of war 85
    Royal Air Force (Great Britain) 24, 28, 77, 82–83
    Royal Marines (Great Britain) 24, 83–84
    Royal Navy (Great Britain) 24, 77, 84–85
    vital records of military personnel 70
    War of 1812
        American prisoners of war 85
        court records 97
    War Office apprenticeship records 89
    Waterloo, Battle of, army lists 79
    World War I records 79, 81, 83–84, 87
Militia lists *see also* Military records
    Canada 82
    Connecticut 82
    Great Britain 24, 82

Index to PRO Record Groups

Arranged Numerically